At Issue

| Homeschooling

Other books in the At Issue series:

Alcohol Abuse

Book Banning

Bulimia

Can Diets Be Harmful?

Child Athletes

Date Rape

Does Capital Punishment Deter Crime?

Drunk Driving

Extreme Sports

Human Embryo Experimentation

Is Global Warming a Threat?

Islamic Fundamentalism

Organ Transplants

Pandemics

Policing the Internet

Political Activism

Private Character in the Public Eye

Sexually Transmitted Diseases

Should College Athletes Be Paid?

User-Generated Content

Volunteerism

What Are the Causes of Prostitution?

What Is a Hate Crime?

Will the World Run Out of Fresh Water?

At Issue

Homeschooling

Heidi Williams, Book Editor

GREENHAVEN PRESS

An imprint of Thomson Gale, a part of The Thomson Corporation

Detroit • New York • San Francisco • New Haven, Conn. • Waterville, Maine • London

THOMSON
★ ™
GALE

Christine Nasso, *Publisher*
Elizabeth Des Chenes, *Managing Editor*

© 2007 The Gale Group.

For more information, contact:
Greenhaven Press
27500 Drake Rd.
Farmington Hills, MI 48331-3535
Or you can visit our Internet site at http://www.gale.com

LIBRARY OF CONGRESS CATALOGING-IN-PUBLICATION DATA

Homeschooling / Heidi Williams, book editor.
    p. cm. -- (At issue)
  Includes bibliographical references and index.
  ISBN-13: 978-0-7377-3685-4 (hardcover)
  ISBN-13: 978-0-7377-3686-1 (pbk.)
  1. Home schooling--United States. I. Williams, Heidi
  LC40.H6673 2008
  370.04'2--dc22

                                                          2007025680

ISBN-10: 0-7377-3685-2 (hardcover)
ISBN-10: 0-7377-3686-0 (pbk.)

Printed in the United States of America
10 9 8 7 6 5 4 3 2 1

Contents

Introduction   **7**

1. Homeschooling Is Becoming More   **10**
   Common Around the World
   Mary Ann Zehr

2. Homeschooling Endangers Democracy   **16**
   Randall Balmer

3. Homeschooling Does Not   **25**
   Endanger Democracy
   Michael H. Romanowski

4. Homeschooling Should Be Regulated   **29**
   Rob Reich

5. Homeschooling Should Not Be Regulated   **43**
   Isabel Lyman

6. Homeschool Partnerships Benefit   **48**
   Public Schools and Families
   Bradley K. Barrett

7. Homeschooling Is Good for Families   **53**
   Blythe Brown

8. Homeschooling Is Not the Right Choice   **58**
   for Every Family
   Dawn C. Pitsch

9. Homeschooling Is a Feminist Act   **63**
   Cheryl Lindsey Seelhoff

10. Homeschool Students Excel in   **70**
    National Competitions
    Andrea Neal

11. Homeschool Students Excel in College   **79**
    Brian D. Ray

12. The Claim that Homeschool Students   **88**
    Excel Is Exaggerated
    Dennis J. Willard and Doug Oplinger

13. Homeschooling Will Change the Future   **99**
    of Education
    Robert Sanborn, Adolfo Santos, Alexandra L.
    Montgomery, and James B. Caruthers

Organizations to Contact   **107**

Bibliography   **111**

Index   **117**

Introduction

In the United States, parents have won the right to homeschool their children in all fifty states, and this social movement is growing faster than ever. A study by the National Center for Education Statistics (NCES) released in 2003, estimated there are 1.1 million homeschoolers in the United States, about 2.2 percent of all school-aged children, up from 1.7 percent in 1999.

At the heart of the "right to homeschool" movement is the issue of parental rights. As Rob Reich, a political science professor at Stanford University explains, many homeschooling parents "view the education of their children as a matter properly under their control and no one else's. They feel entitled to 'purchase' the education environment of their children from the marketplace of learning materials, with no intermediary between them and their child."

Indeed, homeschooling advocates openly make this claim. Michael P. Farris, co-founder of the Homeschool Legal Defense Association (HSLDA), writes about parents' right to homeschool saying, "Parents should have a prior right to make such decisions that is superior to any claim of government."

Parents themselves echo this sentiment. In a focus group conducted for the *Akron Beacon Journal*, several parents asserted that the U.S. Constitution protects their right to homeschool. One parent stated, "I don't take government money. I have a right to raise my kids the way I see fit."

Some people question whether parents' wishes should be the final authority in deciding how children should be educated, arguing that children have the right to a public education and that home education threatens the very fabric of democracy. The clearest example emerges from Europe where the European Court of Human Rights in September of 2006 upheld the right of the German government to ban home education.

The German court ruled that parental wishes "could not take priority over compulsory school attendance," and that parents do not have an "exclusive" right to lead their children's education. The court maintained that the right of the child to an education and to become part of society supersedes parental rights and that "safeguarding pluralism in education . . . is essential for the preservation of the democratic society." In Germany, children have been escorted to public schools by police and even removed from their homes. Sanctions on German homeschooling parents have included fines and jail time.

Some homeschool advocates fear that this decision by the European Court of Human Rights will pave the way to making homeschooling illegal in the United States. Farris believes that if UNICEF's (United Nations Children's Fund's) Convention on the Rights of the Child, which includes the right of every child to an education, were ratified by the Senate or adopted by the federal courts as enforceable international law, American homeschooling could be banned, and warns his readers that "Congressman Jesse Jackson, Jr. (D-Ill.) has introduced a constitutional amendment that declares the right to an education to be the constitutional right of every child."

While supporting parental rights, Reich is concerned about "parents [serving] as the only filter for a child's education" and contends that "students should encounter materials, ideas, and people that they or their parents have not selected in advance."

Many homeschooling parents are diametrically opposed to this view. National figures have openly stated as much. Christopher Klicka, HSLDA's senior counsel wrote in *The Heart of Home Schooling*, "Never become tempted to send your children to public school. It is tantamount to sending your children to be trained by the enemy. If Satan could choose which school system he wanted you to send your children to, he would choose the public school system." Responding to mandated curriculum in California that does not teach that homosexuality is wrong, James Dobson, founder of Focus on the Family, stated on a national radio program, "In the state of California, if I had a child there, I wouldn't put the youngster in a public school. . . . I think it's time to get our kids out."

Homeschooling families themselves share the concerns. One family, the Gotches, interviewed by the *Akron Beacon Journal*, stated that one of their reasons for homeschooling was to be gatekeepers for their daughters, ensuring that their girls' values would be the same as theirs. Among other things, they did not want children from divorced and single-mother families to be a negative influence on them. Randall Balmer, author of *Thy Kingdom Come: An Evangelical's Lament*, quotes one homeschooling father as saying, "We're not going to send our kids into the snake pit of the public schools . . . The whole curriculum is designed to turn children against their parents."

Some will say that such views indicate an intolerance of pluralism. Farris disagrees stating, "A government may promote pluralism. But if pluralism and human rights are to mean anything, they must mean that a person may not be compelled to give up his or her individual views in the name of making a pluralistic society."

As homeschoolers grow in number and gain increasing acceptance in the United States, parents do have the right to educate their children at home using the curriculum of their choice. Parents want what is best for their children, and for an increasing number of parents, homeschooling seems to be the best educational choice. The authors in *At Issue: Homeschooling* examine the emerging issues surrounding this social movement and its impact on education as a whole.

1

Homeschooling Is Becoming More Common Around the World

Mary Ann Zehr

Mary Ann Zehr is an assistant editor for Education Week.

Home School Legal Defense Association in Purcellville, Virginia, has spent the last two decades fighting for homeschooling to be recognized by the United States Government. The organization has successfully lobbied for laws to make homeschooling legal and unregulated in the United States. The homeschooling movement is now spreading worldwide, and HSLDA is now helping homeschooling parents in more than twenty-four countries through mentoring, financial support for legal defense funds, and coordination of activism such as e-mail campaigns for or against legislation.

From his cozy home office here, Christopher J. Klicka is dispensing advice to two evangelical Christian ministers who also happen to be home-schooling dads from Japan.

"Never be satisfied with the status quo," Mr. Klicka tells his guests. "Keep pushing for more freedom so that parents can choose the curriculum and when to home-school. We don't want that controlled by the government."

Mr. Klicka, 44, has long been fighting that battle stateside as a lawyer for the Home School Legal Defense Association in Purcellville, Va. Since its founding in 1983, the nonprofit orga-

Mary Ann Zehr, "U.S. Home Schoolers Push Movement Around the World," *Education Week*, vol. 25, January 4, 2006, p. 8. Copyright Editorial Projects in Education, Inc. 2006. Reproduced by permission.

nization run by evangelical Christians has defended families who want to home-school and has lobbied for laws to make home schooling legal and less regulated.

For the past decade, though, Mr. Klicka has been a home-schooling missionary abroad as well. He has visited other countries to help parents set up organizations modeled after the U.S.-based one. According to the association's Web site . . . he or some other of the group's staff or 80,000 members have helped home schoolers in 24 countries.

Mr. Klicka says that while in the past decade some countries—including South Africa and Taiwan—have legalized home schooling, many countries still don't have explicit laws for home schooling, and some countries that have legalized the practice have burdensome regulations. The HSLDA advises home schoolers on how to be better advocates. For example, if the country permits private schooling, Mr. Klicka counsels them to argue that home schooling is a form of private schooling.

Sometimes, the legal-defense association taps into its fund for international support—about $15,000 a year—to subsidize start-ups of legal organizations. Other times, Mr. Klicka raises money from American home-schooling parents to support their counterparts overseas. He has also coordinated campaigns in which American home schoolers have barraged foreign governments with e-mails asking for the passage or rejection of legislation.

'Good Mentor'

Now the senior counsel for the HSLDA, Mr. Klicka serves on the board of home-schooling legal-defense organizations that it helped start in Canada, Germany, Japan, and South Africa.

"Chris was a good mentor, trainer, educator, and encourager," said Dallas K. Miller, a lawyer and the former executive director of the Home School Legal Defence Association of Canada, in Medicine Hat, Alberta.

While home schooling has always been legal in Canada, Mr. Miller said, the HSLDA of Canada has fought regulation of the practice, such as requirements that local school officials approve the curriculum. The organization has also battled intervention by social-service workers in home-schooling families' lives, he said.

[S]ome 300 Japanese families—about a third of them Christian—teach their children at home, stemming, they say, from the bullying and extreme competition in Japanese schools.

Mr. Miller said he learned legal strategies from Mr. Klicka. They include, Mr. Miller said, "forcing social workers to verify their allegations and accusations, and protecting the autonomy of the family by not letting the social workers interrogate children against their parents' will." The two lawyers also joined together to give presentations in several Canadian cities . . . .

Seeking Acceptance

On this Saturday in December, while four of the seven home-schooled Klicka children go sled-riding outdoors, Mr. Klicka puts his head together with Haruto Yoshii, the director of a support group for home-schooling families in Tokyo, and Seiji Oyama, a businessman and pastor in the Japanese capital.

The visitors also present Mr. Klicka with a gift: a Japanese translation of his 2002 book, *The Heart of Home Schooling.* Mr. Oyama has translated it from English to Japanese and plans to market the book to Christians in Japan.

Mr. Yoshii and Mr. Oyama estimate that some 300 Japanese families—about a third of them Christian—teach their children at home, stemming, they say, from the bullying and extreme competition in Japanese schools.

As a Christian, Mr. Oyama said, he is also uncomfortable with how Japanese schools teach nationalism. "It's a military style," he said. "You have to sing the national anthem. The content is praising the emperor. He is God."

One of the biggest problems home-schooling parents face in Japan is ostracism by other Japanese, some Christians included, according to Mr. Oyama. He and his wife, Kathy, an American, began home-schooling their four children in California, where they lived for about a decade. A year ago, the family moved to Japan, Mr. Oyama's homeland, where he is the pastor of a church of about 250 members.

The fact that home education is already acceptable in a large, wealthy, and culturally influential nation will lend the practice a good deal of initial legitimacy wherever it travels.

Hiroshi Kamiyo, the education counselor for the Embassy of Japan, in Washington, said that the Japanese government has no policy on home schooling, but that the constitution says parents have a duty to make sure their children are educated. The government prefers Japanese to send their children to public or private schools, he said, but won't force them to do so. "So far, our government [education] policy is focused on other areas, like how to address absenteeism or dropouts, or violence and bullying," he said. "These are more serious problems."

Although religion is a prime reason to home-school in the United States, that's often not the case elsewhere, according to a special issue on home schooling that the British journal *Evaluation and Research in Education* published last year. Paula Rothermel, a researcher at the school of education at the University of Durham in England, found only about 4 percent of the 412 British home-schooling families she surveyed said religion was a motive for home schooling. Nearly 31 percent cited disappointment with regular schools.

Schooling in Secret

The special issue describes research on the modern home-schooling movement in Australia, Britain, Canada, Germany, Israel, South Africa, Sweden, and the United States. In the last five to 10 years, the number of homeschooling families has increased dramatically in North America and in Great Britain and other countries, writes David Galloway, the journal's acting editor, in the special issue.

The home-schooling movement in the United States—including the HSLD—has helped pave the way.

Ms. Rothermel writes in reference to the United States: "The fact that home education already is acceptable in a large, wealthy, and culturally influential nation will lend the practice a good deal of initial legitimacy wherever it travels."

That doesn't seem to have helped yet in Germany, where, according to Thomas Spiegler, a researcher in the department of sociology at Philipps-University Marburg, home schooling remains illegal.

"Compulsory school attendance exists in Germany, and home schooling is not allowed," he writes. Mr. Spiegler estimates that about 500 children are home-schooled in Germany "in secret, with tacit toleration by the local authorities or with legal consequences, ranging from a fine to partial loss of child custody, or even the possibility of a prison sentence."

One leader of that country's homeschooling movement is Richard Guenther, an evangelical Christian and the director of a legal-defense organization founded five years ago. Mr. Klicka organized American home schoolers to raise $100,000 for the organization, and he serves on its board.

"We are in quite a cultural war here in Germany," Mr. Guenther said in an e-mail to *Education Week* last month. Our organization "has been very busy in the courts representing families who only want to apply their constitutional rights to educate their children at home, thus protecting them from the liberal agenda being foisted upon them by the government schools."

Officials at the German Embassy in Washington defended their government's position on home schooling. "The public has a legitimate interest in countering the rise of parallel societies that are based on religion or motivated by different worldviews," they said in a statement.

Mr. Klicka said that he and other American homeschooling parents can relate to what the German families are going through, and that's what motivates them to want to help.

When he began working for the HSLDA, home schooling was legal in only five states, some parents who taught their children at home were fined, and government officials sometimes threatened to take their children away. The time: 1985.

2

Homeschooling
Endangers Democracy

Randall Balmer

Randall Balmer is professor of American religious history at Barnard College, Columbia University and visiting professor at Yale University. He is editor-at-large for Christianity Today *and has published ten books, including* Mine Eyes Have Seen the Glory: A Journey into the Evangelical Subculture in America, *which was made into a documentary for PBS.*

An increasing number of Christian parents, encouraged by leaders of the Religious Right are abandoning public education in favor of homeschooling. Children pulled from public schools, whether enrolled in privately-funded or voucher-supported religious schools, charter schools, or educated at home by their parents, miss a key component of public education: learning to co-exist in a democratic society. Furthermore, if the trend away from public schools continues, the expertise of educators will give way solely to religious organizations, big business, or parents; equal educational opportunities will no longer exist and socio-economic segregation will intensify.

For many evangelicals, responding to the litany of complaints from the Religious Right, public schools no longer [seem] tenable. On the eve of the first 1988 presidential primary, I spoke to a young couple in New Hampshire. "We're not going to send our kids into the snake pit of the public schools," the father hissed. "The whole curriculum is designed to turn children against their parents." They chose instead to educate their children at home.

Aside from religious schools and (where available) charter schools, many evangelicals have turned to homeschooling in an effort to flee public education. In 2003, about 1.1 million children (up 29 percent from 850,000 in 1999) were educated at home in the United States, and 72 percent of parents who homeschool their children list "the desire to provide religious or moral instruction" as one of the factors in their decision. Lawree and Scott MacDonald of Antioch, California, for instance, pulled their teenage daughter out of public school late in 2001. The home environment, the mother told *Christianity Today*, is "safer both morally and socially."

As public, or "common," schools took hold in the early decades of the nineteenth century, they became vehicles for social and economic equality . . . .

Public Education Condemned

The drumbeat of criticism emanating from the leaders of the Religious Right has also convinced many evangelicals of the dangers of public education; many have even grown suspicious of the one virtue that has always been the key to the success and the longevity of America's experiment in pluralism: toleration. Leaders of the Religious Right have expressed their disdain for toleration and for pluralism itself, but none rivals James Dobson, head of Focus on the Family.

Dobson's comments about toleration and public education sparked a brief conflagration in 2002. In his March 28 radio broadcast, he said, "In the state of California, if I had a child there, I wouldn't put the youngster in a public school." Dobson objected to what he described as "homosexual propaganda" that children were allegedly being subjected to in public schools; the issue, in fact, was an initiative in California to teach schoolchildren tolerance of others. "I think it's time to get our kids out," Dobson declared.

Dobson's statement attracted a flurry of attention in both evangelical and neoconservative circles. Several months later, according to *Christianity Today*, Dobson reiterated his warning that "this godless and immoral curriculum and influence in the public schools is gaining momentum across the nation in ways that were unheard of just one year ago." He expanded his condemnation beyond California to the states of Connecticut, Massachusetts, Minnesota, New Jersey, Washington, Wisconsin, and Vermont, and to Washington, D.C., all of which he criticized for their "safe schools" law that prohibit discrimination against homosexuals.

Conservatives Agree

Dobson's statements were immediately applauded by conservatives who had been pushing for the end of what they derisively call "government schools." Marshall Fritz, head of the Alliance for the Separation of School and State, with offices in Fresno, California, issued a statement: "With today's courageous and insightful statement, Dr. Dobson joins the millions of Americans who have already discovered that the public schools have become government indoctrination centers which are no place to train new generations of freedom loving Americans." Michael Farris, general counsel of the Home School Legal Defense Association and president of Patrick Henry College, chimed in: "Jim Dobson has always been a leader with courage and those who take a courageous stand on an issue need encouragement." Laura Schlessinger, a conservative talk-radio psychologist, also declared her agreement. "I stand with Dr. James Dobson," she said several days later.

The Importance of Public Education

The Heritage Foundation, a conservative think tank that pushes for taxpayer-funded school vouchers and charter schools, including those run by religious groups, argues that the "battle over who should control America's schools is a battle for the future of our nation." On this point, at least, the Heritage Foundation is absolutely right. Throughout American history, public schools have played a formative role in American society. Following the English Conquest of New Netherland in 1664, for example, the Church of England established an English-speaking school, Trinity School, in New York City to compete with the Dutch school. So effective was Trinity School in altering the ethos of the colony that by the middle of the eighteenth century, Dutch church officials appealed to the Netherlands for an English-speaking minister; the younger generation could no longer understand Dutch.

As public, or "common," schools took hold in the early decades of the nineteenth century, they became vehicles for social and economic equality, as well as for the inculcation of morality and the virtues of citizenship in the new nation. Protestant religious leaders recognized the importance of these schools. In Kentucky, for instance, the first three state education superintendents were ministers. Sheldon Jackson, a Presbyterian missionary, served as the first general agent for education in Alaska, and Samuel Lewis, Methodist lay minister, filled a similar post in Ohio. Another Presbyterian minister, William Holmes McGuffey, who was also a professor at Miami University in Ohio, compiled a series of graded readers, known as *Eclectic Readers*, which taught generations of schoolchildren religious, ethical, and moral principles.

Public schools have played an invaluable role by providing a common ground for children of different ethnic groups and religious persuasions, regardless of social class. In a pluralistic society, public schools provide an opportunity to explore differences and form friendships. At school, children interact with one another and, in the best of all worlds, learn to understand one another and to tolerate one another. Whatever common culture we have attained in this country has come about largely through the agency of public education. At the risk of sounding mawkish, I truly believe that public schools served to make America what it is by helping us forge a mutual understanding of one another as Americans.

The Future If Public Schools Are Abandoned

Homeschooling, school vouchers, and charter schools all diminish the possibilities for such understanding. The private and specialized schools envisioned by the advocates of school vouchers and charter schools threaten that heritage and strike at the heart of the formative mechanism essential for the function of citizenship. By siphoning students from the public schools, private education inevitably narrows that meeting ground.

It also contributes to a ghetto mentality—socially, intellectually, and culturally. The creation of religious schools leads to heightened segregation of different racial and socioeconomic groups. The so-called "school choice" initiative is both a civil rights and a social justice issue, and real Christians, those who take seriously the teachings of Jesus, should be fighting against voucher programs and charter schools because they perpetuate divisions, rather than reconciliation, within society.

The collusion of business interests and the interests of the Religious Right on the matter of public education should make us suspicious.

Indeed, the overwhelming irony surrounding the school-voucher movement is that it purports to be a conservative movement, and it certainly enjoys the support of many political, religious, and cultural conservatives. Yet, the balkanization that follows from the implementation of school vouchers and the formation of charter schools essentially ratifies the most sinister effects of postmodernism and deconstruction by dividing American society into religious, ethnic, economic, and special-interest groups, thereby tearing the fabric of American culture, and identity.

Current Reform Misguided

I don't deny that reform is needed in America's public schools. Violence is rampant, and academic achievement has declined. Children have ever-shrinking attention spans in the age of television and video games. School administrators contend with balky unions; teachers face recalcitrant bureaucracies, and many of the most talented ones finally give up and pursue other, more lucrative careers.

The Bush administration's "No Child Left Behind Act" merely exacerbates the crisis of public education. The emphasis on standardized testing virtually compels teachers to "teach to the test," which, as any educator knows, is a pedagogical strategy utterly inimical to learning. An even more cynical reading of the bill, one advanced by Jonathan Kozol, an educational expert and a former public school teacher, is that the legislation was designed to accelerate the demise of public education. "The kind of testing we are doing today is sociopathic in its repetitive and punitive nature," he told the *New York Times Magazine* in 2005. "Its driving motive is to highlight failure in inner-city schools as dramatically as possible in order to create a ground swell of support for private vouchers or other privatizing schemes." It's quite possible that what Kozol describes is an unintended consequence of "No Child Left Behind," but the deleterious effects of the bill cannot be ignored.

A Suspicious Alliance

The collusion of business interests and the interests of the Religious Right on the matter of public education should make us suspicious. In the end, the war on public education is about money—the huge opportunities for profiting from parents' fears of secular education. In its war against public education, the Religious Right has allied itself with affluent Americans already paying for private education and with anti-government, free-market conservatives who support vouchers and charter schools for very different reasons, to advance their own political and economic agendas.

But this thinking is shortsighted, and it abandons the crucial task of intellectual and social formation to capitalists. In an address before the convention of the National Association for the Advancement of Colored People in 1999, Reg Weaver, an African American and vice president of the National Education Association, pointed out the obvious: If capitalists are supporting school vouchers, the scheme is probably not calibrated to the best interests of education. "If most minority children, children of color, children of disadvantage and poverty, are going to have any chance at a quality education," Weaver said, "they aren't going to get it from big business, they aren't going to get it from the tender mercies of the free market, and they sure aren't going to get it from the scheme cooked up by the far right. They can, however, get it from a reformed and revitalized—a redeemed—public education system."

A Critical Situation

The future of American democracy hangs in the balance in the tussle over homeschooling, school vouchers, and public education. The large and growing movement toward private education and homeschooling represents a betrayal of an essential component of American culture, and I find it paradoxical that the very people who purport to reclaim America's past are the same people seeking to jettison such a key and formative institution in America's history. Public education, and the underlying conviction that schools are important gathering places, is central to our identity as Americans: public schools provide the most logical place, perhaps the only place, where future generations, especially within a pluralistic context, can coexist with at least a measure of comity and learn the rudiments of democracy. Whatever their shortcomings—and I don't want to understate those shortcomings—

public schools can and must be preserved. If we care anything about democracy, we must care a great deal about public education.

No Quick Fixes

In the face of overwhelming deficiencies in public education, school vouchers and charter schools sound like a quick fix. They rescue us from the hard work and the difficult choices required to reclaim the proud and distinguished legacy of public education in America. But school vouchers are chimerical, especially in an age where we face, more directly than ever before in our history, the challenges of pluralism. Now is not the time to encourage the balkanization of our schools and, by extension, our society.

The school voucher discussion will not abate soon. The Supreme Court's unfortunate five-to-four decision in 2002 to approve the voucher plan in Cleveland handed the enemies of disestablishment the victory they had long sought. The issue is now in the hands of state legislators, who must make the appropriations for school vouchers and the provisions for charter schools. Still, those who value the First Amendment and public education cannot afford to be complacent, in part because the voucher proposal has the potential to unite two constituencies into a powerful coalition: religious conservatives, on the one hand, and those who already send their children to nonreligious private schools, on the other. The appeal for the former group is obvious: Why not have your religious convictions supported financially by the government, even if this threatens the First Amendment proscription against established religion?

The latter group finds vouchers attractive because they would offset the expensive tuition costs they are already paying for private schooling, as the experience in Ohio demonstrates. These people, by and large, are more affluent and can afford these tuitions, so why should the government subsidize them, especially when that money could be helping to educate those less privileged? If the neoconservatives and the Religious Right have their way, "government schools" will disappear altogether, and learning will take place in the home, in voucher schools run by religious groups, or in charter schools operated by capitalists.

I can't imagine anything less democratic.

3

Homeschooling Does Not Endanger Democracy

Michael H. Romanowski

Michael H. Romanowski is a professor at the Center for Teacher Education at Ohio Northern University in Ada, Ohio.

The homeschooling movement has been accused of endangering democracy by producing politically and socially isolated citizens. Recent studies dispel this myth by demonstrating that homeschooled graduates are more civically active and contribute to society more significantly than graduates of public schools. The parents' right to make decisions for the best interest of their children is the hallmark of a truly democratic educational system.

In August 2001, *Time* magazine raised the issue of citizenship and homeschooling by asking the question, "Is Home Schooling Good for America?" The concern was that homeschooling may turn out better students, but does it create better citizens? The argument was that homeschooling isolated students from the world, including political and social involvement. Furthermore, homeschooling centers on the best interest of the individual rather than public schools' concern for the best interest for society as a whole.

Today, the first generation of homeschooled students have grown up and have entered America's workforce, colleges, and universities. But, are they good citizens compared to the gen-

Michael H. Romanowski, "Revisiting the Common Myths about Homeschooling," *The Clearing House*, vol. 79, January–February 2006, pp. 125–129. © 2006 Heldref Publications. Reproduced with permission of the Helen Dwight Reid Educational Foundation, published by Heldref Publications, 1319 18th Street, NW, Washington, DC 20036-1802.

eral U.S. population? A recent report, "Home Schooling Grows Up," released by Dr. Brian Ray, argues that "home schooling produces successful adults who are actively involved in their communities and continue to value education for themselves and their children." The study surveyed more than seventy-three hundred adults who were homeschooled, with more than five thousand of these being homeschooled for at least seven years. Their responses and results demonstrate that homeschooled students are excellent citizens compared to the general U.S. population.

Active Citizens

For example, one element of being a good citizen is a person's level of engagement in civic and political affairs. According to these findings, only 4.2 percent of homeschool graduates consider politics and government too complicated to understand, compared to 35 percent of U.S. adults. Ray demonstrates that homeschool graduates are more actively involved in their communities than the general U.S. population. The following statistics illustrate this point:

- Seventy-one percent of homeschool graduates participate in an ongoing community service activity, compared to 37 percent of U.S. adults of similar ages.

- Eighty-eight percent of the homeschool graduates surveyed are members of an organization (such as a community group, church, or professional organization) compared to 50 percent of U.S. adults.

- Homeschool graduates are more likely to contribute money to a political party and are more likely to work for a political party or cause.

- Seventy-six percent of homeschool graduates surveyed between the ages of eighteen and twenty-four voted in a national or state election within the last five years,compared to only 29 percent of the relevant U.S. population.

- Homeschool graduates are more likely to have participated in a protest or boycott, attended a public meeting, wrote, or telephoned a public official or signed a petition more often than the general population. The bottom line: Homeschool graduates are actively involved in the political process and are more engaged as citizens compared to the general U.S. population.

As educators and community members, we need to respect parents' choices because this is the essence of a democratic educational system.

These findings dispel the myth that homeschoolers withdraw from society and their civic responsibilities. Homeschoolers clearly learn about the real world, possibly more than do their public school counterparts. While the purpose of public education is to educate future citizens who take an active role in improving the social, economic, and political conditions in society. Ray's research indicates that public schools, not homeschooling, should be scrutinized for their efforts regarding "citizenship training."

Responsible Citizens

What about other aspects of adulthood, such as employment? [J. G.] Knowles surveyed adults who were homeschooled because of ideology or geographical isolation. None were unemployed or on welfare. Nearly two-thirds were self-employed. In addition, 94 percent of those surveyed stated that their home education prepared them to be independent persons, while 79 percent said it helped them interact with individuals from different levels of society. Knowles argues that because such a large percentage of those surveyed were self-employed, this provides evidence that homeschooling develops an individual's self-reliance and independence.

It seems that homeshooling creates responsible and productive citizens, which is positive for both the individual and society. Children are benefiting from the homeschool environment and much can be learned from examining what homeschooling families are doing. . . .

Working Together

The essence of a public school system in a democratic society is that the educational system listens critically to the concerns of parents and provides avenues for parental choice. More important, the expectation that public education should adequately serve the needs of children from broad and diverse backgrounds should be reconsidered. Public schools do not, cannot, and probably should not be expected to meet the needs of every child in the community. Instead, parents, schools, and the community need to work together to educate all children, no matter what form of education parents choose. Our main concern should be that education, whatever form it takes, maximizes the potential of all children. Inevitability, this will lead some parents to select alternative and less institutionalized options for their children's education. As educators and community members, we need to respect parents' choices because this is the essence of a democratic educational system. Instead of constantly comparing and contrasting public schools and homeschools, we should look at how each can learn from one another and then use this information to improve the learning experiences of all children, no matter what form of education takes place.

4

Homeschooling Should Be Regulated

Rob Reich

Rob Reich is an assistant professor of political science and ethics in society at Stanford University. He is the author of Bridging Liberalism and Multiculturalism in American Education.

Homeschoolers, whether left-wing unschoolers or right-wing religious fundamentalists, agree that homeschooling should be unregulated; however, no reliable research has been conducted to examine the outcomes of a typical home education. Simply pointing to inadequate public schools is not a valid argument for unregulated homeschooling. While parents have the right to homeschool their children, the state has the responsibility to protect the freedom of its citizens, including children. Homeschool regulations are necessary to ensure that children learn basic skills and how to participate as citizens in a diverse democracy.

Everyone now knows that home schooling has gone mainstream in the United States. Once a fringe phenomenon, home schooling is legal in every one of the 50 states and is widely considered the fastest growing sector of K-12 schooling. Because education in the United States is a matter delegated to the states—the U.S. Constitution does not mention education—each state has different provisions for regulating home schooling. This patchwork regulatory environment shows a clear trend across the country, however: regulations

Rob Reich, *Homeschooling in Full View: A Reader*. Charlotte, NC: Information Age Publishing, 2005. Copyright © 2005 by Information Age Publishing. Reproduced by permission.

that 30 years ago either forbade or strictly regulated home schooling have been lifted or eased. According to the Home School Legal Defense Association (HSLDA), an advocacy group for home schooling that has been instrumental in getting more permissive home school legislation passed in many states, 25 of the 50 states have no regulations governing home schooling except a requirement that parents notify a local public authority that they have set up a home school. Ten of these 25 states do not even require parental notification.

Home schoolers are now a diverse population. No longer the preserve of left wing unschoolers and right wing religious fundamentalists, the great range of people who have chosen to home school their children make it very difficult to draw even broad generalizations about the phenomenon. Indeed, it is easy to observe a kind of internecine warfare among the two most prominent advocacy groups, the Christian-based HSLDA and the more secular and inclusive National Home Education Network (NHEN). Nevertheless, one article of faith unites all home schoolers: that home schooling should be unregulated. Home schoolers of all stripes believe that they alone should decide how their children are educated, and they join together in order to press for the absence of regulations or the most permissive regulation possible.

[T]o say that people need permission to home school because the public schools are woeful is a red herring.

Home schooling should be a permissible educational option, but I believe that home schooling must be strictly regulated. In this chapter, I shall discuss and defend the need for regulating home schooling far beyond the measures taken in most states today. Regulations are necessary for a number of reasons. These reasons can be usefully classified under two separate headings: theoretical and evidentiary. I proceed by arguing for the theoretical and evidentiary basis for regulating home schooling, and I conclude with a provisional list of appropriate regulations.

The Home School Debate

Let me begin, however, by identifying two very common pitfalls in debates about home schooling. First, arguments in favor of regulating home schooling are not hidden arguments about the virtue of public schools. Nothing I write here is a defense of public schooling in the United States. Indeed, I have argued elsewhere about the need to provide new options to children who are forced to attend failing public schools, and I have defended a version of a school voucher system that would radically reorganize the current system of public education in the U.S. Moreover, my experience with home schoolers leads me to believe that the availability of high quality public schools in their neighborhood would not motivate the vast majority of them to send their children into the public school system; they home school for different reasons. Thus, to say that people need permission to home school because the public schools are woeful is a red herring.

Second, arguments about regulating home schooling ought not be a war of conflicting anecdotes about home schooling's glorious successes or horrible tragedies that so often make headlines in the United States. To promote unregulated home schooling on the basis that home schooled children often win the National Spelling Bee and annually win coveted admissions spots to Stanford and Yale is poor argumentation. It is equally poor argumentation to defend regulations on home schooling because several children each year are found starved, abused, and even killed by their home-schooling parents. These extreme and unrepresentative cases—both positive and negative—ought not to be the basis of policy-making, and they distort the public representation of and debate over home schooling. Conservative estimates place the number of homeschooled students in the United States at 1.1 million in 2003. It is the vast middle that is worth discussing, the children who do not enroll at Stanford and who have loving, caring parents.

Theoretical Arguments for Regulating Home Schooling

Home schooling is the education of children under the supervision of parents. In no other educational setting are parents as able to control and direct all aspects of education, for in home schools they are responsible for determining not only what children are taught, but when, how, and with whom children are taught. Home schooling therefore represents the apogee of parental authority over schooling. Unregulated home schooling is nothing less than total and complete parental authority over schooling. The theoretical arguments for regulating home schooling begin from this point, questioning whether the schooling of children should ever be under the total and complete control of parents.

Some will find this a tendentious way of framing the question. Parents, they will say, are the appropriate authority over their children. What needs defending is not parental authority over schooling but whether the state should have any authority over the upbringing of children. So let us ask two separate, but related questions: What justifies, if anything, government authority over the education of children?; and what justifies parental authority over the education of their own children?

It is important here to recognize that parents ought indeed to possess wide-ranging authority to raise their children as they see fit, including wide-ranging discretion over the education of their children. This is so for many reasons, chief among them that parents are responsible for the care of their children and that they know their children better than anyone else. Let us take it as given, therefore, that parental authority over their children is legitimate and desirable.

What reason is there, then, to think that the government ought to have any authority over the education of children, an authority that could in certain circumstances curtail the authority of parents? I think there are two answers to this question. Call the first the "citizenship argument" and call the second the "freedom argument." The citizenship argument seeks to justify providing children with a civic education and thereby avoid the development of civically disabled adults. The freedom argument seeks to justify providing children with an education that cultivates their freedom and thereby avoid the development of what I will call "ethically servile" adults. Together these arguments justify some state authority over the education of children and rule out total parental control of education.

Children are the youngest citizens of the state, and the state has an interest in assuring that children receive a civic education.

Citizenship Argument

The citizenship argument is the most familiar reason for justifying state regulation of schooling, and for this reason I shall only provide the barest outline of it here. Versions of it can be found in a number of important Supreme Court decisions and in state laws governing education. . . .

Children are the youngest citizens of the state, and the state has an interest in assuring that children receive a civic education. Citizens are created, not born. And though people differ about what it means to be a citizen and can argue a long time about the catalogue of civic virtues it is proper to instill in children, the point I make here is merely that the state has a legitimate interest in trying to convey some basic ideas about citizenship through schoolhouses.

It needs to convey basic facts—the structure of government, some rudimentary history. And it needs to convey some basic procedures about political participation—that being a citizen carries certain ground rules, such as one person, one vote, that no citizen can be excluded from the political process simply because he or she has different beliefs, or differently colored skin. Finally, the state needs to ensure that basic literacy and numeracy is learned so that children can become self-sufficient, productively employed citizens, not relying on the state—that is, on the taxes of other citizens—for support. In short, the state is justified in requiring that all children—regardless of the school they attend, public, private, or home school—receive a civic education.

Freedom Argument

The freedom argument is more complicated and less evident in legal and legislative history. In this sense it is more speculative. Nevertheless, it is the heart of the moral argument that I believe is most compelling when we consider the need to regulate home schools. Begin from the first principles of a democratic state. One of the chief aims of a democracy—especially a *liberal* democracy, where liberal is understood in its classical not contemporary and partisan sense—is to protect the freedom of individuals. One of the salutary consequences of a liberal democracy that protects individual freedom is that the choices individuals make about how to lead their lives leads to social diversity, or value pluralism. It would be shocking if in a society that protected the freedom of individuals it turned out that everyone believed the same thing. Simply put, protecting the freedom of individuals is the main engine of diversity—diversity of religious belief, diversity of belief in general.

Limits to Freedom

Under what circumstances should freedom be limited? The standard classical liberal response is that liberty should be restrained when the exercise of one person's liberty interferes with or harms another person. This is generally called the "harm principle" among philosophers. The liberal democratic state can legitimately pass laws that restrict your liberty to harm other people.

What is key to understand is that liberal democracies enshrine the individual, not groups or collectives. Each child is an individual, and while no liberal democrat wants children to have the same legal or political status as an adult, the fact remains that children have the same interest in freedom as adults do. That is, children are born to freedom, though are not born in the condition of being free.

With little or no exposure to . . . people whose convictions differ from their parents', children who are home schooled can be raised in an . . . environment that fails to develop their capacity to think for themselves.

The liberal democratic state therefore ought to protect the interest of children in being free, or as I have put it elsewhere, in becoming autonomous adults. The interests of children are separable from the interests of their parents, and the interests of children in becoming free or autonomous—in becoming self-governing and self-determining persons—are as important as the interests of parents in being free or autonomous. Thus, the freedom argument is at bottom about ensuring that children acquire the capacity to lead the lives they wish, to believe what they want to, and to be free, when they become adults, from the domination of other people and institutions (from their own parents as well as from the state). In other words, I seek to prevent both governmental and parental despotism over children, even a benevolent, loving despotism.

Education Encourages Autonomy

What does this have to do with home schooling? The answer is that one of the most effective and least intrusive ways the state has of discharging the obligation to protect and promote the prospective freedom of children—a freedom that they will exercise fully as adults—is to ensure that children receive an education that develops them into free or autonomous individuals, that is to say, persons who can decide for themselves how they wish to lead their lives and what sort of values they wish to endorse. Such an education, I believe, requires exposure to and engagement with value pluralism, the very social diversity that is produced in a liberal democratic state which protects individual freedom. Unregulated home schooling opens up the possibility that children will never learn about or be exposed to competing or alternative ways of life. Home-schooled children can be sheltered and isolated in a way that students in schools, even sectarian private schools, cannot be. Parents can limit opportunities for social interaction, control the curriculum, and create a learning environment in which the values of the parents are replicated and reinforced in every possible way. With little or no exposure to competing ideas or interaction with people whose convictions differ from their parents', children who are home schooled can be raised in an all-encompassing or total environment that fails to develop their capacity to think for themselves. . . .

Children Must Be Free Persons

Let us be honest about the implications here: protecting and promoting the prospective freedom of children by providing them an education that exposes them to and engages them intellectually with the diversity of a pluralist democracy can be threatening to parents. The social critic bell hooks has written of her own childhood, for example, "School was the place of ecstasy—pleasure and danger. To be changed by ideas was pure pleasure. But to learn ideas that ran counter to values and beliefs at home was to place oneself at risk, to enter the danger zone. Home was the place where I was forced to conform to someone else's image of who and what I should be.

School was the place where I could forget that self and, through ideas, reinvent myself." But these are risks that must be accepted, for children have an interest in being free persons and parents cannot be entitled to ensure that their child grows up to be exactly the kind of person they want her to be.

Thus, the freedom argument leads to the conclusion that the education of children ought to be regulated in such a way as to guarantee that they learn about and engage with the diversity of ways of life in a democracy. Receiving such an education is one very important way the state can attempt to protect and promote the future freedom and autonomy of children. It is also important, I would add, for civic reasons that go beyond what I described in the section above. The reason is that citizenship in a culturally and religiously diverse liberal democracy requires that each citizen be prepared to recognize that the values that guide his or her life will not be shared by all other citizens. Therefore, each citizen needs to learn to be able to participate democratically with citizens of diverse convictions.

The justification of state authority over the education of children is rooted in developing children into citizens (or avoiding civically disabled adults) and in developing children into free persons (or avoiding ethically servile adults). This is the structure of the theoretical argument that warrants regulation of home schooling.

Evidentiary Arguments for Regulating Home Schooling

Home schoolers and the mainstream media have publicized the idea in recent years that the academic performance of home-schooled students is better or equal to that of publicly schooled students. Advocates have used various studies to reach the conclusion that home schooling works. But contrary to popular opinion, very little if anything is known about the actual academic performance of the typical home-schooled student, the vast middle that I suggested ought to be the appropriate basis for debates about home schooling. Research on home schooling is in its infancy and what little research currently exists is either of poor quality or is capable of reaching only very limited conclusions. As a result, the very best we can say about the academic outcomes of home schooling is that we have no evidence to suggest that home schooling fails. But neither do we have any evidence that it succeeds.

One would think that the increasing number of home schoolers would attract the interest of both social scientists and policy makers. Home-schooled children, after all, are a larger population than the number of children who attend charter schools, a phenomenon that receives extraordinary attention from researchers, public policy makers, and the media. Why is it that home schooling is so little studied? A large part of the explanation has to do with resistance from the home-school community and the unregulated nature of the enterprise.

Home Schooling Data Is Imprecise

Start with one of the biggest problems: the fact that we have no accurate data on what one would think is the truly easy question, the number of children who are home schooled. The U.S Department of Education study referenced earlier is the most scientifically rigorous and most conservative, pegging the number at 1.1 million in 2003. Brian Ray of the National Home Education Research Institute (an advocacy organization, not an impartial research institute), however, estimates the number at 1.7 to 2.1 million. The variation in estimates here is unusually wide. How can it be that the data is so imprecise? A simple answer emerges. Because home-schooling regulations are either so minimal or so little enforced, many parents do not notify local educational officials when they decide to home school. Recall that 10 states do not even require parents to register their home schools. A great deal of home schooling occurs under the radar, so to speak, so that even if local officials wished to test or monitor the progress of home-schooled students, they would not even know how to locate them. Researchers and public officials have, quite literally, no sense of the total population of home-schooled students. This is the primary obstacle to studying home schooling.

In order to be sure that home-schooled children, who have no opportunity to protest or seek academic assistance elsewhere, do not suffer educational harm, home schools must be regulated.

A further concern is that an appalling amount of the research conducted on home schooling and given publicity in the media is undertaken by or sponsored by organizations whose explicit mission is to further the cause of home schooling. . . . Of course, that research is conducted by persons whose pay comes from organizations dedicated to promoting home schooling is no reason to reject the findings out of hand. I would suggest, however, that we treat the findings of their research on home schooling in the same way that people treat the research on nicotine addiction funded by tobacco companies: with a very large dose of skepticism. . . .

Reliance on Anecdotes

Absent rigorous, social scientific data on the outcomes of home schooling, we are left in the realm of glorified anecdote—the home schoolers who win the National Spelling Bees—and the occasional ethnographic study of small populations of home schoolers. But neither can give us any picture of whether home schooling works. The very best research on home schooling—the combination of random samples of large populations and ethnographic studies, yields some good information about the reasons why people home school and demographic characteristics of their households. But when we look at the academic performance of home-schooled children, the bottom line is that we know virtually nothing. . . .

I wish to make my point very clear here. I do not suggest that home-schooled children do worse than publicly or privately schooled children. I do not accuse home-school parents of failing to teach their children well. I want to say simply that we know almost nothing about how the average home-schooled child fares academically.

Why does an absence of evidence about the academic outcomes of home schooling lead to an argument in favor of regulating home schools? Children whose parents fail to teach them to read and to write, to be capable of minimum basic skills, are suffering educational harm. In order to be sure that home-schooled children, who have no opportunity to protest or seek academic assistance elsewhere, do not suffer educational harm, home schools must be regulated. . . .

A Provisional Regulatory Framework for Home Schooling

I propose three minimal regulations. The results of the democratic process might yield additional regulations, which would not necessarily be inconsistent with my views, but these seem to me the bare minimum, as follows:

1. All parents who home school must register with a public official. The state needs to be able to distinguish between truants and home-schooled students, and it needs a record that specific children are being home schooled so that its other regulations can be enforced.

2. Parents must demonstrate to educational officials that their home-school curriculum meets some minimal standard. The minimal standard will include academic benchmarks as well as an assurance that children are exposed to and engaged with ideas, values, and beliefs that are different from those of the parents. For instance, every home-school curriculum should include

information about a variety of religious traditions. (I believe this should be the case, as well, for public and private schools.) Parents are free to teach their children that their own religious faith is the truth, but they cannot shield children from the knowledge that other people have different convictions and that these people are, from the standpoint of citizenship, their equals.

3. Parents must permit their children to be tested periodically on some kind of basic skills exam. Should home-schooled children repeatedly fail to make progress on this exam, relative to their public or private school peers, then a case could be made to compel school attendance. Label this educational harm. (The same kind of educational harm surely exists in some public schools, of course. And this is one reason that I believe parents should have the authority to hold the state accountable for its public schools by pulling their children from failing schools and enrolling them elsewhere.)

In short, these regulations amount to the following:

- The state registers who is being home schooled.

- The state insists upon a curriculum that meets minimal academic standards and that introduces students to value pluralism.

- The state tests students periodically to ensure that minimal academic progress is being made.

Would many home schools be unable to meet these regulations? I suspect not that many, but I do not really know the answer to the question. It is worth finding out. As I have endeavored to show, it is both theoretically and practically necessary to regulate home schools. If creating and enforcing regulations would prevent even a few children from suffering educational harm or from receiving an education that stunted or disabled their freedom, the regulations would be worthwhile.

Strictly enforced regulations ensure that parents do not wield total and unchecked authority over the education of their children. What is at stake here is not a question of social utility or stability, whether home schooling could threaten democracy. What is at stake is the justice that we owe children, that they receive an education that cultivates their future citizenship, their individual freedom, and that teaches them at least basic academic skills, skills that are necessary for ably exercising both their citizenship and their freedom.

Homeschooling Should Not Be Regulated

Isabel Lyman

Isabel Lyman is a columnist and author of The Homeschooling Revolution. *She also homeschooled her two sons.*

In the United States, some state legislators are pushing for more oversight and regulation of homeschools to the dismay of many homeschooling parents, students, and advocates who believe that such oversight is unnecessary, disruptive, and a violation of their rights. As the number of bills introduced in state legislatures increases, so does the fervor of the grass-roots opposition, which is well-organized and largely successful.

"There's no place like home" has become the mantra of successful homeschoolers. By most measures—scholastic, social, economic—the modern homeschooling movement is a triumph. The actual undertaking requires initiative, patience, and, in many cases, financial sacrifice. But this grand educational adventure continues to work because resourceful homeschoolers have largely been left alone.

Unfortunately, it is the "home alone" aspect that scares opponents, who waste precious human resources criticizing this successful private-sector, parent-managed endeavor. Meanwhile, thousands of ill-supervised children have languished, decade after decade, in public schools.

Rob Reich, a Stanford University assistant professor of political science, is one such critic. In a paper entitled "Testing

Isabel Lyman, "Keeping Homeschooling Private," *The New American*, vol. 19, September 8, 2003, pp. 27–28. Copyright © 2003 American Opinion Publishing Incorporated. Reproduced by permission.

the Boundaries of Parental Authority over Education: The Case of Homeschooling." Reich states, ". . . I argue . . . that at a bare minimum one function of any school environment must be to expose children to and engage students with values and beliefs other than those they are likely to encounter within their homes. Because homeschooling is structurally and in practice the least likely to meet this end, I argue that while the state should not ban homeschooling it must nevertheless regulate its practice with vigilance."

This attitude is seen in the resolution passed by the Representative Assembly of the National Education Association (NEA). Last July, at their annual summer convention, the NEA passed Resolution B-69, which states that "home schooling programs cannot provide the student with a comprehensive education experience."

But the NEA cannot begin to inflict the same kind of damage on homeschoolers as can zealous state officials. Phonics specialist and homeschooling advocate Samuel Blumenfeld has observed: "Today the law is not being used to force delinquents and truants into the schools, but to harass and regulate home schoolers. . . ." In Blumenfeld's home state of Massachusetts, Kim and George Bryant, homeschooling parents, endured a seven-hour standoff with police officers and social service employees merely because the Bryant children—teenagers Nicholas and Nyssa—declined to take a standardized test ordered by the Department of Social Services.

Revolt In the Constitution State

Like minutemen of old, homeschooling families must also be ready to fight unexpected assaults on their rights. For example, last year in Connecticut, home educators challenged the Act Concerning Independent Instruction, which contained a tedious list of new mandates, including ones requiring homeschooling parents to possess a high school diploma, as well as have their individual curriculum plans scrutinized by school superintendents.

The *Hartford Courant* reported that state Rep. Cameron Staples (D-New Haven), the act's sponsor, championed this proposal because in Connecticut "the only law on home schooling requires parents to let local school districts know that they plan to teach their children at home." Apparently, this approach was too *laissez faire* for the lawmaker, and one wonders what Staples would do if he were in Oklahoma, where there is no requirement for parents to initiate contact with the state if they choose to homeschool their children.

Staples and his ilk, however, were probably not expecting scores of parents to challenge his clumsy attempt to increase homeschool regulations. Diane Connors, president of the Connecticut Homeschool Network, sent an e-mail to parents and other concerned citizens, alerting them to the public hearing regarding the bill. Her dispatch was wildly successful. On March 4, 2002, over 1,000 people—many coming from the Legislative Office building in Hartford—attended the hearing to voice their opposition to the House version of the act. According to Connors, only one Connecticut superintendent showed up to support the legislation.

Summarizing the prevailing sentiment against the bill, homeschooling parent John Paradis was quoted in the *Courant* as explaining, "We have removed our kids from the public schools because we think the public schools are not educating our students properly. This [the bill] puts their education back in the hands of the public schools."

Legislators didn't ignore the outcry. On March 22, 2002, [the bill] died, missing the deadline for receiving a favorable vote.

Big Sky Showdown

Even though no evidence exists indicating that state regulation improves homeschoolers' performance, legislators continue their campaigns to control and restrict home education. This year, another showdown—like the one in Connecticut—occurred in Montana.

State Senator Don Ryan (D-Great Falls) sponsored Senate Bill No. 276. If the legislation passed, it would have required homeschoolers to take state assessment tests to measure academic competency. Even though Montana is a state with an undemanding existing homeschooling law and where homeschoolers had outperformed public school students on national standardized tests, the responsible were to be penalized. Ryan, employing the emotional language of left-wing children's rights advocates, said he was concerned about protecting at-risk children from "inadequate" or "abusive" parents.

On February 12, 2003, hundreds of Montana homeschoolers, alerted by phone and e-mail chains by another attentive parent (Steve White, the legislative liaison for the Montana Coalition of Home Educators), converged on the capitol in Helena to lobby against the bill. The arguments the Senate Education Committee heard ranged from the unfairness of testing homeschoolers on material they had not studied, to being held to higher standards than their lower-performing public school counterparts, to concerns about state infringement on teaching religious beliefs.

Homeschooling works best when it is left alone.

The hearing lasted a record four hours, and nearly 500 Montana citizens signed the hearing registry as opponents of the bill. Home School Legal Defense Association (HSLDA) lawyer Dewitt T. Black wrote in an e-mail alert that "over 50 people testified against it." Only one person—Senator Don Ryan—spoke in favor. The education committee voted 9-1 to "postpone indefinitely," ensuring that S.B. 276 was dead on arrival.

Never-Ending Battles

J. Michael Smith, president of HSLDA, notes that his organization lobbied against a cache of bad bills during the 2002-03 school year. "We had nine states where there were specific threats to home school freedom that we lobbied: Montana state assessment test required for home schools; North Dakota state assessment test; Nevada state assessment test; Wyoming state assessment test; California habitual truants would be treated as educational neglect; Texas would have required registration of home schoolers; Colorado habitual truants would be treated as educational neglect; Louisiana attempted to do away with private school exemption for homeschoolers; and Virginia wanted home schoolers to pass the standards of learning tests given to public school students. None of these bills were successfully passed."

Clearly, some state legislators are trying to regulate a nonexistent problem. These lawmakers are trying to hinder, not help, the vast majority of homeschoolers. They are also unprepared to deal with the fierce opposition and almost zero public support that their meddling produces.

The only assistance state lawmakers can offer home educators is to deregulate homeschooling—eliminate cumbersome laws and not introduce new, costly legislation. Some states are catching on. The opening of a story from the *Oakland Tribune* was pleasantly surprising: "Just nine months after declaring homeschooling largely illegal, the California Department of Education recently reversed its position, pronouncing the practice as essentially none of the state's business." The California Department of Education, in fact, has begun referring interested parties to statewide homeschooling organizations to receive their information.

Frederic Bastiat, the 19th-century French economist, could have been writing about deregulating homeschooling when he opined, "It [the law] can permit this transaction of teaching-and-learning to operate freely and without use of force. . . ." Perhaps more American legislators will get the message: Homeschooling works best when it is left alone.

6

Homeschool Partnerships Benefit Public Schools and Families

Bradley K. Barrett

Bradley K. Barrett is superintendent of the Gilbert Unified School District 41 in Gilbert, Arizona.

Taking advantage of liberal charter school laws enacted in 1994, thousands of families in Arizona have left public education for homeschooling. When the homeschooling movement proved more than a passing fad, educators in some districts successfully implemented state funded partnerships that provide programs offered specifically to homeschooled students. The partnerships benefit homeschooling families and also build bridges between public and home educators.

Ever since I took my first administrative position in the central office in Gilbert, Ariz., in the late 1970s, parents have become less timid about voicing their concerns to educators. Twenty years ago parents had few options other than hoping their local public school leaders could be influenced to accommodate their unique concept of elementary or secondary education.

We in education were confident in our efforts to resist any change, given our status as the only game in town. We were the experts and dismissed many parents as arrogant and unenlightened. We did it our way and the public could take it or leave it. In Arizona, parents were not necessarily encouraged to leave public education, but state politics made it easy to do.

In those days, family flight from the public schools was not a big concern for me and my colleagues in school district administration. First, I knew the vast majority of parents would stay loyal to their neighborhood school. And by all statistical measures their children were receiving a decent education with which no one could compete.

Permissive Laws

Then things changed. Under the charter school law passed in 1994, Arizona became known as the "education of choice" state. This distinction has resulted in 430 charter schools and more than 14,000 home-schoolers statewide. Arizona has made it painless for parents to home-school with little need to document their effectiveness or be held accountable for the progress of their students. In our state, public education flight is a reality and a concern.

As parent after parent asked for a type of education we felt was outside our philosophical ability to deliver, we allowed them one by one to leave our district to establish schools in garages, living rooms and rented office space. As they left I said goodbye to neighbors and many good friendships established over the years. Emotionally it was difficult to see them go. Intellectually I knew they would soon return to public education.

The Exodus

To my surprise, however, they didn't come back. Instead they lobbied the state legislature for more liberal laws to accommodate their beliefs and their desire for greater influence in their children's schooling. This continued for more than a decade until the 1990s when I left Gilbert to assume the superintendency in nearby Kyrene School District, which had been experiencing the same exodus of students to non-public education.

Thousands of parents had given up on the public school system and were taking advantage of state laws to educate their children as they pleased. It is difficult to know how many students (and therefore how many dollars) are leaving a district because records of students being educated in alternative settings are not easily obtained.

Alternatives

After more than three decades in this profession, my views about the role public education should play in the lives of students changed. I became annoyed at the word "charter" because I believe the charter of educating America's children belongs to the traditional public school and it is our charter to lose. Yet charter school parents and home-school parents alike pay taxes to maintain public education in the district of their residence. I now have come full circle and believe that public schools should reach out to families using alternative schooling, particularly home-schoolers, to offer whatever resources we have to better educate our students.

To that end, a few years ago I met with several home-schooling parents to explore how we might assist them in educating their children—assuming they could surmount their strong personal feelings about public education. We had educational resources to enrich the curriculum they were teaching and professional materials to increase their effectiveness at home as they struggled with some of the same issues we deal with in the public school classroom.

My feelings after that first meeting were mixed. Some parents chose to continue their distrust of public education. A few were excited about the possibility of enhancing their children's education and their own teaching skills by partnering with the local school district.

An Experimental Partnership

At the time we happened to have an unused section of a newly built school. Eventually it would be filled but for a couple of years we could devote several classrooms to the home-school/public school partnership. We met with the home-school parents to determine what enrichment curriculum would be meaningful to them. We agreed their students could benefit from computers, foreign language, art, music and library access. We also invited them to look at our curriculum materials.

The benefits ... go beyond the enrichment experiences that home-schoolers experience in public schools.

We informed the home-schooling parents all of this was available to them at no cost because the state would reimburse us for the time spent in our schools. We assured them their children did not have to associate with other students in the school but would have access to all of our equipment whenever they desired. We also developed a schedule to accommodate their needs.

The home-school partnership program began with 80 elementary students participating. As that number increased gradually, we added a second facility.

A Relaxed Hard Line

I since have returned to Gilbert Public Schools as superintendent. This was the site where 20 years earlier as associate superintendent I first experienced student migration when my philosophy was not as accommodating. Knowing of our track record in Kyrene, home-schooling parents in Gilbert approached me upon my return. Consequently I met with the home-school community once again to determine the parents' interest in partnering. As in Kyrene, we wanted to serve as a resource to parents and to assist with the professional issues of home-schooling their children. Many, not surprisingly, are interested in the opportunities we can offer.

My role as a superintendent is to provide a quality education to any student who wants to be part of the public school environment. At this point in my career I am confident in accommodating other educational philosophies that I might not choose for my own children and providing home-schooling parents with a quality public education at whatever level they desire. The benefits derived from this go beyond the enrichment experiences that home-schoolers experience in public schools.

Even those who do not take advantage of our services are softening their antagonism against public schools because of their interaction with home-schooled families who've had positive experiences in our schools. I only regret I came to this realization relatively late in my career.

7

Homeschooling Is Good for Families

Blythe Brown

Blythe Brown is a family physician in Calgary, Alberta.

Homeschooling allows parents to spend more time with their children and to customize their children's education. Support is available from many venues, but the venture still demands lifestyle changes and income adjustments. The results are academically prepared, well-adjusted kids and closer family bonds.

Why would someone of semi-sound mind and body want to homeschool their kids? Especially medical doctors: Don't we have enough to do? Aren't there schools to take care of that sort of thing?

My wife, Marina, and I are both family physicians. We homeschooled our four children for six years, including kids in kindergarten to grade nine, and had a fantastic family time. We still worked more than half-time (which amounts to what most would call full-time), and enlisted Grandma and Grandpa to fill in the slack.

The Requirements

To be an expert homeschool teacher, the job description is long, but the qualification list is short. As with most things, it helps to have a burning passion for the subject, in this case our kids. We knew we were naturals for the job because we're enthusiastic, hard-working and excellent at Trivial Pursuit (except the entertainment category). That plus the fact we love learning and attended 17 years worth of university between us means we might have learned something useful to pass on.

The Reasons

Why did we homeschool? In our case, we thought it would be a good challenge and a way to really know our children. Sort of like an elite private school with a favorable teacher-to-student ratio. Nevertheless, the biggest reason was it was fun!

We travelled a lot. Three months in Australia allowed us to explore the geography, geology, flora, fauna and even literature, to a depth found in first-year college programs. The kids remember it to this day because they experienced it first-hand. Trips to the jungle, catching a moray eel on a fishing rod, sticking a flipper into the gaping mouth of a giant clam, playing bell with a kangaroo—we never could have had those kinds of experiences in Canada as busy family physicians with kids in public school.

We created many memories, such as the homeschool presentation on giant squid, which ended with serving the audience a sample of cooked squid prepared by our 11-year-old. There was the Greek model with the little multicoloured period figurines, fired in a kiln followed by a menu written in Greek. We even did a history of medicine. I learned a lot.

Mind you, to this day, our youngest child hates jellyfish after a bluebottle managed to wrap its tentacles around her ankles. Nevertheless, she knows to pee on it to neutralize the burn!

A relatively new phenomenon, the number of homeschooled kids in Canada is growing rapidly every year. It hasn't always been so. Not so long ago, you would risk truancy charges and possibly even jail if you kept your child in homeschooling. Our homeschool supervisor (you need one) was one of the first homeschool parents in Saskatchewan. It was an uphill legal battle all the way.

There are many other reasons to homeschool. One common reason is related to religious beliefs. We learned that creation, the theory of evolution and the age of the earth are quite emotional topics.

The Curricula

Where did we begin? While it helps to have a big enough family for a basketball team, four kids were enough to make us feel our time was well-used.

There are support groups everywhere, offering practical advice on different curricula, book resources, co-operative learning ventures and field trips. Most valuable of all, there are discounts from many different bookstores, including wholesale library suppliers.

Most universities now offer continuing education courses relevant to homeschoolers. We heavily utilized the Calgary Public Library, which had wonderful, new, inviting books. We found the maximum number of books we could sign out on one card is 99! We needed a used clothes hamper to get them all home. We also learned they accept Visa for late fines.

Local homeschooling associations got us started. They filled us in on registration with a sponsoring school district, so we didn't get into trouble with the local laws regarding truancy and mandatory schooling.

I was amazed to learn how efficient we were compared with a normal school.

The best curriculum was our own interest-based curriculum, as well as a combination of several commercially available courses of study. We added a few modifications of our own. This involved picking any subject we really wanted to learn about, finding out as much as you could, then reading, writing, drawing, acting and generally ferreting out as much information and experience on the subjects as humanly possible.

The Lifestyle

It does require a certain amount of devotion and a major shift in lifestyle and income. We had to ask ourselves how much money we needed to survive. Try juggling a doctor's career so he or she can still see a cadre of patients in the office in two fewer days per week, and still be available the rest of the week to admit to the hospital, be on call and carry the overhead, if required. It was not easy and required much finagling and fine-tuning. We made sure we had at least one and often two locums [someone who substitutes temporarily for a member of the same profession] to cover office patients when we were not there. More than once, we left the kids at McDonald's with a few bucks while we went into the hospital to attend to an emergency.

It was kind of a romantic lifestyle, like being medical missionaries in the Amazon, or living in a remote lighthouse on the West Coast. The big event in the fall was when the giant canvas bag arrived loaded with curriculum and supplies sent as part of our commercially available study course. It was ripped open like Christmas parcels and was filled with books, CDs, even scribblers, pencils, erasers and rulers.

[T]hese were some of the most rewarding and enjoyable years of our lives.

I was amazed to learn how efficient we were compared with a normal school. It is a well-kept secret that school can be taught in three days a week—easily. I found we could teach the core curriculum, as required by law, in the length of time it took us to drive the kids to school. The extracurricular fun stuff like sports and music were in the afternoons. We had nights off.

A typical day in the life of a homeschooler would look something like this: traditional subjects in the morning (we would work anywhere—maybe in the living room, around the kitchen table, in the rec room, even on the deck), followed by a picnic lunch on the hillside inside a teepee ring or the old sandstone quarry. Then in the afternoon we would dump off a couple of kids for piano lessons and guitar, take one grocery shopping (which also turns into an impromptu lesson in budgeting, home economics and the Canada food guide). One afternoon each week, we went to the Winter Club. There the kids could partake in tennis, squash, badminton, swimming, skating—you name it. Afterward we could prepare a family meal, or my wife and I could actually take time as a couple to go out on a date.

The Results

Everyone except homeschoolers seems to worry about socializing. Well, kids do just fine. With the extra lessons at the club, Scouts, Brownies, Sunday school, music, family events and travel, their socialization was quite complete. Homeschooling is about divergent, interest-based learning with a variety of age groups.

As homeschoolers, we were often concerned how our children would hold up academically. On average, homeschoolers perform 15% to 20% above their peers on SAT exams; some of the more enlightened post-secondary institutions hold open special positions just for homeschoolers. They tend to do very well in university, as they are self-directed learners.

Homeschooling is not for everyone. However, these were some of the most rewarding and enjoyable years of our lives. You learn your children's unique gifts and learning styles. No one takes his or her interest and passions to heart as much as you can.

If you are thinking about it, take a risk. Just do it. You won't regret these days together. Those kids aren't little forever.

8

Homeschooling Is Not the Right Choice for Every Family

Dawn C. Pitsch

Dawn C. Pitsch is a writer and former homeschooling mother.

Some parents underestimate the challenge of homeschooling. When children are younger, the task is easier, but as children get older, the lessons require more preparation. Also, developmentally, the social needs of children increase as they mature. Even when both parents and children are unhappy, parents may pressure themselves to continue homeschooling. While homeschooling is a good choice for some families, it is not one size fits all. The value of stepping back and reevaluating the homeschool experience as it applies to your own family cannot be underestimated.

It was a typical homeschooling day. My 8-year-old, Jason, walked into the living room and saw me reading the morning paper.

He scowled. "What are we going to do today? Nothing, as usual?"

The accusation stung. "We do lots of things!" I insisted.

"Not every day!" he fired back.

My son was right. Although I had good intentions, my teaching was inconsistent at best. *How did it get like this*? I wondered.

Dawn C. Pitsch, "I Was a Homeschool Dropout: I Thought Teaching My Kids at Home was the Best Thing for our Family. But God Had Another Lesson Plan.," *Christian Parenting Today*, vol. 16, spring 2003, p. 56. Copyright © 2003 by Dawn C. Pitsch. Reproduced by permission of the author.

The Dream

From the time they were babies I knew I wanted to teach Amanda and Jason at home. Kids taught at home reportedly did better academically, outpacing other students on standardized tests. They also showed better self-esteem because they were less peer-oriented than kids in school. Best of all, homeschooling meant my husband and I could transmit our values to them without competition from New Age philosophies or humanistic views. How could I not do something that promised so much?

I began researching methods, and heeding the best advice I could find. I developed a customized approach that practically guaranteed success. We didn't do "school" every day, so I had time to run errands, do housework, or visit friends—no burnout for me! We joined a support group and enjoyed field trips and classes with other families—we'd never feel isolated. I based our curriculum on my children's strengths and interests—they'd love learning.

Sure enough, things went well at first. I loved teaching Amanda and Jason to read, and they were eager learners. I was sure we would turn out the kind of children any parent would want: smart, confident, and self-motivated.

But there were problems ahead.

The Reality

As the kids got older and there was more to teach them, staying prepared grew more difficult. I began to dread getting out of bed in the morning for another day of school. Many days we really did end up doing nothing. To make matters worse, I took their progress personally. After all, I was the teacher. If they didn't succeed, it was my fault!

It was no picnic for my children, either. I drove Amanda to tears of frustration with my unrealistic demands. "Why don't you know how to spell that?" I'd scold. "You just had it on your test last week!" When she had to take her first standardized test, Amanda was so anxious she refused. The idea of being timed and evaluated stressed her out so much she ripped up the answer sheet and fled to her room.

Meanwhile, Jason and I clashed almost daily. Although Jason was an excellent reader, he didn't enjoy reading like I had as a child. Strong-willed, he wanted to do his schoolwork in his own way, and as fast as possible so he could go play. His sloppy handwriting drove me crazy. When I'd correct his inventive ways of forming certain letters, he'd tell me, "This is the way I do it." I had no authority as a teacher.

My disappointment was immense. Where were the eager, self-directed learners I'd read so much about? These two acted like normal kids. My passion was gone, too. I'd been so certain this was the right choice for us, but now I just wasn't sure.

All the way along our homeschooling road, I'd sought the advice of friends. Some encouraged me to stick it out and try new techniques. Others, though, questioned my decision to homeschool. A teacher friend told me, "I could never teach my daughter. Our personalities clash too much." I could relate, but didn't want to let go of my dream of a happy homeschooling family. My husband's grandmother wrote me a letter saying things like, "They need someone else to teach them," and "They need to be away from you for part of the day." I thought, *She just doesn't understand. I want to be sure my kids live for the Lord, and this will guarantee it.*

Hanging On

Even as it became clear that we were failing, I held on tighter. I felt like I had to prove to the world and myself that I could do this. *Homeschooling seems so right for so many families, I'd tell myself. Surely it's right for mine, too.*

Every few months I'd read about a new product for spelling, or math, or science, and excitedly buy it. Often the change of material renewed our interest, but it also caused a lack of continuity, and a lot of holes in my kids' education.

Jason began asking to go to school, blaming me for his having no friends.

I prayed for God's help, and often felt him nudging, "Trust me. Send them to school." My husband, Neal, believed the kids would be fine in public school, but I was still afraid to give up control. So I redoubled my efforts. I'd read another book, go to a new seminar, talk to a homeschooling friend, all to convince myself that I was doing the right thing.

Then reality hit. Their first "official" test scores came in. They were so bad that I knew the kids needed to go to school. But how could I send them when they were so far behind? The teachers would know I was a fraud. I'd give all the other homeschoolers a bad name.

The final problem was social. Homeschool advocates say kids don't need to go to school for social interaction, and that may be true for many kids. But my kids were lonely. They had lots of contacts, but not many close friends. They had a few friends at church, but they didn't live close by. Jason joined a homeschool band in the sixth grade, but only saw those kids two hours a week. He didn't have any neighborhood friends, and was often bored and angry. I felt worn out trying to or-chestrate social activities for him.

Jason began asking to go to school, blaming me for his having no friends. Amanda was apathetic. She didn't want to learn at home, but she wasn't sure she wanted to go to school, either.

I can't begin to describe my relief at finally letting go.

God continued to whisper, "Let go." I continued to re-sist—so much so that I began to have stomach problems.

Then one day I wandered into a Christian bookstore, and found a new book on homeschooling. I thumbed through it, wondering if I might find something new. I did. The author firmly believed in homeschooling but said that each of us needs to be sure of our calling. God may even have us teach our kids for a time, and then call us to send them to private or public school.

Letting Go

This was unusual, coming from a committed homeschool mom. But I saw it as an answer to my prayers. In the weeks to come, I began talking to Christian parents I knew who had kids in the middle school in our area. They had no reservations about the education their children were receiving. Neal and I decided to meet with the school's principal and were impressed with her values. We registered the kids for the fall.

I can't begin to describe my relief at finally letting go. For the first time in years, I felt close to the Lord again. I'd been shutting out his voice for so long I couldn't remember how good it felt to follow him. I'd forgotten that even my best intentions can turn sour when they aren't in line with where God is leading me.

The results have been incredible. Amanda and Jason are both doing well in school. Many of their friends are Christians, and they care about seeing their non-Christian friends saved. They have both been able to explore their own interests and talents without me hovering over them. Amanda has found her niche in art, and Jason in music. We discovered that we are a family that needs some time apart. Now we enjoy each other so much more.

Each morning as I say good-bye to my college freshman and high school senior, I am so glad I trusted God and let them go. He has a plan for their lives, and I am allowed the joy of watching it unfold. I like that so much better than trying to direct it myself.

9

Homeschooling Is a Feminist Act

Cheryl Lindsey Seelhoff

Cheryl Lindsey Seelhoff is former publisher of Gentle Spirit *magazine and creator of* Women's Space, *a blog space for radical feminists.*

A feminist movement to redefine motherhood and family life has been underway for over 40 years now. The decision to homeschool or unschool children, as an individual family or as a feminist community, is central to this revolution. This lifestyle empowers women and families and allows for the creation of community, varied learning experiences, creative family businesses, and shelter from male supremacy and negative socialization.

A revolution in motherhood and family life has been underway for over 40 years now. It is a revolution I have had a part in creating and which I helped to lead, and which has consumed the better part of my time and energy for the past 35 years. Quietly, ordinary women like me have been recreating, reinventing motherhood, family life, our own lives, as well. I wonder why the revolution we are making has, by and large, been so invisible, and how the trails we've managed to blaze for ourselves might be broadened so that other women can, if not walk alongside us immediately, at least see the trailheads, beckoning them. I hope this article will be a step in that direction. . . .

The journey . . . has changed me. . . . It set me on a course towards revolutionary feminism, for one thing. It opened to me the possibility for radical, nonhierarchical parenting. It taught me the errors of coercion. It broadened my hopes and vision for women's space, women's land. Above all my experiences taught me that it was possible to create a new and better life, even within the constraints of a surrounding male supremacist culture.

What is exciting and inspiring to me is, this is not a life reserved for the privileged. Along the way I have met and come to love so many people, from all races, ethnicities, religions, classes, homeless people, differently-abled people, single mothers, lesbians, who have embarked on this same journey and who love it just as I do.

I could write many books—and may!—about the specifics of the revolution I have participated in making. In this essay I can provide a beginning place for women interested in a radically different motherhood experience, a vision of the trailhead, where the path begins.

Education

The most revolutionary decision I made when I left my career was to home school, and later unschool, my children. (Unschooling is a term coined in the late 1970's in the United States to describe learning centered on a child's interests and needs. Instead of beginning with parents' or educational experts' ideas about what is important to learn, unschooling begins with a child's natural curiosity and expands from there. Unschooling does not mean that children are not taught by parents or others; it means that parents and others make sure that when the child is ready and interested in exploring or learning, she has access to the resources she needs.) This was 1983, a time during which it was illegal for children to be home schooled in my state. I worked together with other parents lobbying state legislators to pass a bill which would allow parents to home school. Over the years, similar bills were enacted in all 50 states, and now many millions of children are being home schooled.

Imagine a world in which children are free to unfold and learn in their own time and way. Imagine freedom from school schedules and school activities, including the freedom to travel any time of the year, to sleep when it makes sense and to work and study when it makes sense. Imagine being free to pack up the kids and attend a demonstration or rally on a moment's notice. Consider deciding, together with your children, what kind of history, science, art, literature, poetry to study or learn or create. Consider providing a woman-centered education, unhindered by the regulations of the patriarchists, from the time your child is born. Imagine all of the many hours you would not have to spend confronting racism, sexism, misogyny, classism or bullying in the schools, whether at the hands of children or teachers or other staff. Imagine a world in which, as Sonia Johnson describes, children were spared the "soul-killing, joy-destroying agents of patriarchy . . . especially the public schools."

I have now been home schooling my children for 23 years. There are thousands of us, progressive, creative, highly educated, artistic people living this lifestyle. The decision to "teach my own" has been central to the motherhood revolution I am describing.

Community

Removing children from public schools allows for the creation of community with others who share your values and lifestyle. Freed from the tyranny of school and work schedules, like-minded feminist women can find one another, teach their children together, schedule outings, trips, vacations any time of year. They can garden together, protest together, serve in the battered women's shelter together, create feminist girls' organizations, teach classes cooperatively, create vegetarian food

co-ops, . . . raise farm animals, create art and music, participate in sports, raise money for worthy causes, volunteer at the
local abortion clinic, animal shelter, or homeless shelter. These
activities are not the province of women who have degrees or
money or who own their own homes or property only. All of
these and many more activities, projects and endeavors are
possible for all kinds of families, including single moms living
in apartments.

---

*Whatever happened to feminist notions of communities,
including communities of women, loving and raising
children together?*

Imagine raising children who need never be scarred or
traumatized by the dehumanizing effects of such things as
popularity and beauty contests, proms, school bullies, peer
pressure, including the pressure to conform to gender stereo-
types, to be "feminine" or "girly" or "macho," religious bigotry,
religious holidays, homophobia, racism, or exposure to gangs,
drugs, alcohol or weapons at school. Envision instead deciding
with your children where and how they will learn about all of
these things.

Child Care

I am with Sonia Johnson in the belief that left to ourselves,
feminist mothers would never have made child care as we
know it today any sort of priority or issue. Daycare as it exists
in this culture usually amounts to the warehousing of the
smallest, most vulnerable human beings with all of the atten-
dant risks and dangers. Rejection of daycare centers as a priority does not mean agreeing that the work of care giving belongs to mothers only. Whatever happened to feminist notions
of communities, including communities of women, loving
and raising children together? My own view is that given,
again, the tyranny and rigid regimentation of modern life un-

der Western male supremacy, feminist women simply couldn't figure out how to create these nourishing, life-giving communities, and so the beautiful ideas were forgotten, rejected as impossible, impracticable. But what if communities of women were organized to, among other things, share in the raising and nurturing of children, with adults teaching their children cooperatively, caring for them together, and making provisions for breaks and times of solitude and respite for each mother in the community? Clichéd though it may be, it really does take a village to raise a child; if we do not create our own "villages," we are stuck with those which are and will be forced on us via public education, sports, neighbors, daycare centers. As women we are so often impoverished in that we have not been able to carve out space and time to create such nourishing villages. I have experienced community life and know enough of it to say with confidence that there is no better context for the raising of children than a community of like-minded women who love and respect both children and one another.

Nonhierarchical Parenting

My mothering journey led me to parenting nonhierarchicaly and noncoercively, relying on negotiating win/win solutions to conflicts and difficulties, as opposed to relying on rules, hierarchies, "discipline," for dealing with conflicts in my large family. This style of parenting, so consistent with historic feminism, is made difficult wherever the lives of mothers and children are regulated by the demands of school and work schedules. It is a revelation where it is practiced in the context of supportive intentional communities.

Work

Home schooling families have often worked hard to create their own businesses which they operated from home. Over the course of my own home schooling I have been a vendor at the local farmer's market, have raised organic gardens, sheep for wool, and chickens for eggs, have made and sold dolls, soap, herbs, and herbal products, have written for publication and spoke at conferences. In 1989, I began a 'zine hoping to connect with other mothers who shared my values and lifestyle. I began it with 17 subscribers; within five years I had 30,000 readers internationally and published a full-color glossy magazine 11 months of the year. My publication supported my large family for most of 11 years. The magazine was not only my family's source of income, it also provided opportunities for my children to be mentored in publishing. Through the years of the magazine's publication, my children wrote and edited articles, created graphics, proofread, and performed office and administrative work depending on their ages, gifts and interests.

There are many successful home business stories in the home schooling community, where families have created books, magazines, pamphlets, curriculum materials, support organizations, or have offered various kinds of services to their communities. There are also home schooling families in which both parents work, as well as families in which single mothers home school. In single-parent families, mothers sometimes care for and teach one another's children while the others are at work.

This lifestyle offers amazing opportunities for separatist feminists interested in creating intentional communities.

Then, too, in general, home schooling is conducive to a very simple lifestyle. The pressure for school clothes and ongoing expenses of activities and school projects is eliminated, along with transportation expenses and the expenses of school lunches. Where moms work from home, the same is true; there is no need for a wardrobe for work, for bus fare or carfare, and of course, there are no daycare-associated expenses.

Where families are home- and community-based, via food co-ops and other kinds of sharing and co-operating, many kinds of expenses can be kept to a minimum.

Radical Feminist Separatism

This lifestyle offers amazing opportunities for separatist feminists interested in creating intentional communities. It is possible given this kind of lifestyle to organize all of one's life, activities, and spending around women, women's concerns, women's politics, woman-owned businesses and organizations. One of the most-often-heard objections to the kind of lifestyle I have described is that it might not prepare children "for the real world." My response, always, is to ask, . . . whether this is something that, as feminists, we really want to do, whether raising children who fit in nicely with the "real (male supremacist) world" is consistent with our feminism, or just with our deepest values as feminist mothers.

I have been in the process of raising six daughters and five sons over these past 35 years. I have three children still at home, eight grown now, and I am a grandmother to four, two of whom are being unschooled as their parents both were. One of the most gratifying outcomes of my experience of motherhood is the determined radical feminism of every one of my daughters and the support for feminism of my sons. . . .

My deepest hope is that feminist women will not settle for less than revolution, will not return to the traditions and lifestyles of pre-feminist times, but will join with me and mothers like me in the revolution we have been engaged in, now for decades.

10

Homeschool Students Excel in National Competitions

Andrea Neal

Andrea Neal, former editor of the Indianapolis Star *editorial pages, is a teacher at St. Richard's School in Indianapolis and an adjunct scholar for the Indiana Policy Review Foundation.*

Homeschooling has become so mainstreamed that it is no longer surprising when a homeschool student walks away as spelling bee champion or scholarship winner. Advocates credit individual structure, individualized attention, and a flexible schedule, which allows students to focus on their interests. Once viewed as civil disobedience, homeschooling is now legal in all 50 states, practiced by people of every conceivable religion and background, and is more widely accepted even by those who don't practice it. Studies have found that homeschool students often perform a grade level above their age-level and score higher on standardized achievement tests.

It wasn't so long ago that homeschoolers like Johanna Schilling, Jonathan Gainer and Eli Owens were oddballs in the education landscape. Not anymore.

You name the contest—National Spelling Bee, National Geographic Bee, National Merit Scholarship—and chances are good that homeschool kids have participated, performed with distinction, and won. These days, headlines of academic

Andrea Neal, "Homeschoolers: Into the Mainstream: Excelling in and out of the Home, Homeschooled Kids are Thriving Across the Country," *Saturday Evening Post*, vol. 278, September–October 2006, p. 54. © 2006 Saturday Evening Post Society. Reproduced by permission.

achievement are as likely to feature homeschooled children as their peers from traditional public and private school settings. Perhaps just as noteworthy, nobody's jaw drops when it happens.

This year, four homeschooled students were named semifinalists in the Presidential Scholars competition, which recognizes the nation's most distinguished high-school graduates. The honor served notice of two important trends: one, homeschoolers have entered the mainstream of academic achievement; two, they're being recognized for it.

Success Stories

Stories abound of homeschoolers' success:

At 17, Johanna was recognized as the first homeschool winner of a $40,000 Ruth DeYoung Kohler Scholarship for Artistic Merit in her home state of Wisconsin. She will use the money to pursue her studies at the Houghton College school of music in New York.

Eli, 19, a homeschool graduate who attends West Virginia University, was named a 2006-2007 Goldwater Scholar in March. He was one of 323 college students nationally to receive the award, established by Congress to encourage advanced studies by select sophomores and juniors who excel in math, science and engineering.

Jonathan, 14, was the first homeschooler picked for the Kelley Junior Executive Institute, a summer program at Indiana University that identifies 50 high-achieving, primarily minority high-school students interested in studying business. Note that he's the age of a typical eighth grader, yet he's already completed Algebra II.

These stories are just the tip of the iceberg. In 2005, a homeschooler won the National Geographic Bee. Homeschoolers swept the first three spots in the 2000 National Spelling Bee. In 2003, the latest year for which figures are available, a record 129 homeschoolers were named National Merit Scholars, an increase of more than 600 percent over 1995. The estimated 1.8 million homeschoolers—out of 54 million children in kindergarten through high school—seem to be achieving honors disproportionate to their numbers.

Structure and Small Class Size Spell Success

"It's not surprising that a homeschooler gets much better academic results. There's just no way around the structure," says Ian Slatter, director of media relations for the Home School Legal Defense Association in Virginia.

Yes, structure matters. Although it varies by family, the typical homeschool consists of one parent teaching one or more children in the home. But not just in the home. Homeschoolers take field trips and visit museums and libraries. They network with other homeschool families. They use books and curricula that reflect their own academic and religious values, yet align closely enough to state academic standards that students are prepared for standardized tests, which some states require. In a homeschool, the teacher-student ratio for any given lesson is 1:1 or 1:2. Not even an elite private school, where class size is capped at 16 or 18, can rival that.

Because of structure and flexibility, the typical homeschool student can complete graduation requirements by age 16.

The structure works especially well in the elementary years as students are mastering math and reading skills that will be the foundation for later learning. When course work grows more complex, many homeschool families contract with experts to teach their children more advanced subjects, sometimes pooling resources to create small classrooms not too different from a traditional school.

Flexibility Is Key

It's the flexibility that so many homeschooling families lift up as the key ingredient. In a homeschool, parents can quickly identify a student's areas of strength and weakness, offering enrichment opportunities for the former and focused attention on the latter.

Those with a gift for music can take instrument lessons or catch a symphony matinee when their traditional classmates are in school. Johanna, for example, spent up to three hours a day practicing piano for 10 years. Computer whizzes can seek out apprenticeships with nearby businesses; those who love sports can finish their workout in the morning before the YMCA gets crowded.

Because of structure and flexibility, the typical homeschool student can complete graduation requirements by age 16. As a result, some go to college early; many enroll in local community colleges until their parents deem them ready to live on a campus with older students.

Rough Beginnings

But it's not always been an easy road for families wishing to homeschool. Until recently, state laws and regulations deterred all but the most committed parents from opting out of the regular school system.

Historians trace the modern homeschool movement to the 1960s, when social reformers and counterculture activists questioned the benefits of the conventional school day, with its regimen of discipline and structured learning. That movement was short-lived, in part because it saw itself as a form of civil disobedience, unconcerned with changing laws to facilitate the legal homeschooling of children.

After the Supreme Court struck down school prayer as unconstitutional in 1963, a conservative and explicitly Christian movement arose to pull children out of what was seen as an increasingly secular and valueless school system.

Throughout the 1970s, Slatter notes, homeschooling was essentially illegal in 45 states, where teacher-certification laws permitted only licensed teachers to instruct students of compulsory school age, typically 6 to 16. Slatter's group was formed in 1983 to lobby to change those laws and practices that impeded homeschooling and to help families navigate regulations. By 1993, all 50 states had recognized a parent's right to homeschool.

Growing Support

Around the same time, a homeschooling industry arose offering training programs and curricular materials for families getting started. *Home Education Magazine*, based in Washington state, has been published for more than 20 years and features articles and columns about effective practices. Today, homeschool support groups and Internet-based clearinghouses can be found at the click of a mouse.

Although evangelical Christians remain the single biggest group in the homeschooling movement, they are by no means the only ones. In her book *Homeschoolers' Success Stories*, Linda Dobson notes that "families from every conceivable religious, economic, political, and philosophical background in the United States" have realized the benefits to homeschooling.

"This wave has been impelled by homeschooling's greater visibility as an educational option; local, state, and national homeschooling support groups; easy networking and information sharing via the Internet and e-mail; and continuing government-school problems, such as dumbed-down curriculum, violence, drugs, bullying, and more," she writes.

Slatter, whose group is Christian-based but will assist all home schoolers regardless of faith, says the reasons for opting out of public schools haven't changed much in 20 years. "Consistently, the two top reasons for homeschooling include the negative peer environment of public schools. We're talking about drugs, crime and negative peer influences. There's also the lack of a biblical worldview or any sort of religious teaching. No education is values-free. A public school that is actually going to be teaching will inevitably undermine the religious values parents will be teaching."

A Growing Acceptance

What has changed is public understanding and acceptance of the homeschool phenomenon. The percentage of those feeling that homeschooling is a "bad thing" dropped from 73 percent in 1985 to 57 percent in 1997, according to a Phi Delta Kappa (PDK)/Gallup poll. In a 1999 poll, PDK asked if public schools should make services available to children who are schooled at home, and a surprising number of respondents said yes. The numbers ranged from a high of 92 percent for special education courses for disabled or handicapped children to a low of 53 percent for transportation services.

There are critics, to be sure, including members of the National Education Association, the powerful teachers' union. "Don't most parents have a tough enough job teaching their children social, disciplinary and behavioral skills?" asks one such skeptic in an opinion column posted on the NEA website. Dave Arnold, a member of the Illinois Education Association, suggests it's better to leave formal education to professionals. Parents, he said, "would be wise to help their children and themselves by leaving the responsibility of teaching math, science, art, writing, history, geography and other subjects to those who are knowledgeable, trained and motivated to do the best job possible."

Statistical Support

The data, however, are on the homeschoolers' side.

In the most significant study to date, "Scholastic Achievement and Demographic Characteristics of Home School Students in 1998," researcher Lawrence M. Rudner made the following findings:

- Almost 25 percent of homeschool students are enrolled one or more grades above their age-level peers in public and private schools.

- Homeschool student achievement test scores are exceptionally high. The median scores for every subtest at every grade (typically in the 70th to 80th percentile) are well above those of public and Catholic/private school students.

- On average, homeschool students in grades one to four perform one grade level above their age-level public or private school peers on achievement tests.

- The achievement test score gap between homeschool students and public or private school students starts to widen in grade five.

- Students who have been homeschooled their entire academic life have higher scholastic-achievement test scores than students who have also attended other educational programs.

Smaller studies have affirmed the findings, and Slatter says his organization hopes to do an updated achievement study in the near future.

One Family's Success

Homeschool families are gratified by the research but say the real proof can be seen in their well-adjusted and well-rounded children. Ariana and Jonathan Gainer of Indianapolis are a case in point. Both spent two years in a private school, which they liked; both endorse the flexibility that homeschooling gives them to pursue their passions.

Ariana, 12, loves to read and write. She is active in her church and involved with Y-Press, a news-reporting network that allows young people to experience journalism firsthand and get their work published in the Indianapolis Star. At the moment, Ariana is researching a story on rumspringa, the time when Amish children are released from their church's control to decide if they will accept the faith of their families.

Jonathan envisions a career as a CEO, a dream bolstered by his time at the Kelley School of Business Summer Institute at Indiana University. While there, Jonathan headed up a team of five students responsible for developing a business plan from conception through presentation to stockholders. The team's idea—a cell phone company with global, wireless Internet subscriptions—was researched so well that it won first place in the institute competition. The experience was invaluable, Jonathan says, because he got to work with other students on a team and learn in a more collaborative way than he is accustomed.

Their parents, Marvin and Jerrilyn Gainer, first got a taste of homeschooling when they served as missionaries in Mexico and the children were just preschool age. For Marvin, a stint as a substitute teacher in the Indianapolis public school system solidified his belief that homeschooling would be right for their children.

The Columbine High School shooting rampage had just occurred, and Marvin says he fully understood how it could happen. He recalls "total chaos in the hallways . . . total disrespect students had toward teachers" and the inability of principals to impose adequate discipline to get things under control.

Families Work Together For Success

"There was nothing going on there that impressed me. For a kid to do well in that system, they had to spend so much energy trying to survive. I just didn't want that for my kids."

Now, with their own children thriving, the Gainers have launched an educational center in innercity Indianapolis where homeschooling families can come together for specialized instruction. They seek out the top people in their fields to teach upper-level and Advanced Placement courses, such as etymology, biology and calculus. Families share the costs.

The center creates opportunities for socialization but, better yet, makes available the kind of teaching typically associated with elite private schools. Yes, homeschools have entered the mainstream of America's educational system, and their students intend to compete with the best and brightest in the country.

11

Homeschool Students Excel in College

Brian D. Ray

Brian D. Ray, president of the National Home Education Research Institute (NHERI), has been studying homeschooling for 25 years.

Homeschool students are more than academically prepared for college. They are socially, emotionally, and psychologically developed and show a strong self-identity. They score high on standardized academic achievement tests and on exams that predict college preparedness, such as the ACT and SAT. Home-educated students are, in fact, being recruited by some colleges and universities. College admissions officers need to recognize the validity of a home-education and develop reasonable and fair admissions policies.

Most people know that parent-led, home-based education is neither a new concept nor a new educational practice; it is millennia old. By the late 1970s, however, it was estimated that only 13,000 grades K-12 students were being homeschooled in the United States. The practice of homeschooling was specially rekindled during the 1980s, promoted by individualist parents and educational thinkers with a variety of backgrounds in pedagogical philosophies and religious worldviews. With 1.7–2.1 million K-12 students home educated during the 2002–2003 institutional school year,

Brian D. Ray, "Homeschoolers on to College: What Research Shows Us," *The Journal of College Admission*, no. 184, fall 2004, pp. 5–11. Reproduced by permission.

home-based education is now arguably the fastest-growing form of education, compared to public and private institutional schooling. . . .

Academic Performance Before College

One of the first questions researchers ask is, "Does homeschooling work, academically?" Many policy makers, educators, school administrators, and parents wonder whether ordinary mothers and fathers, who are not government-certified teachers, are capable of teaching their children after age five. Is it possible for adults without specialized, university-level training in teaching to help their children learn what they need to learn?

Many studies have been completed during the past 20 years that examine the academic achievement of the home-educated. Dozens of researchers have executed these studies. Examples of these studies ranged from a multi-year study in Washington state, three nationwide studies across the United States, and a nationwide study in Canada. In study after study, the homeschooled scored, on average, at the 65th to 80th percentile on standardized academic achievement tests in the United States and Canada, compared to the public school average of the 50th percentile.

In study after study, the homeschooled scored, on average, at the 65th to 80th percentile on standardized academic achievement tests.

Researchers, wondering if only certain families—in which the parents have a high educational attainment or family income—are able to homeschool such that their children score high on achievement tests, show that children in homeschool families with low income and in which the parents have little education are scoring, on average, above state-school averages. In addition, research shows that the parents' teacher-certification has little to no relationship with their children's academic achievement, and that the degree of state control of homeschooling (i.e., regulations) has no relationship with academic achievement.

Social and Emotional Preparedness for College

Socialization questions are asked of nearly every homeschool parent and every homeschool teenager. Some of them tire of the questions; others receive them as an opportunity to spread the word about one of their favorite topics. These questions arise mainly in societies in which the institutionalization of children is the norm for children during the ages of six to 18.

More specifically, the first question usually asks if the child will experience healthy social, emotional and psychological development. Numerous studies, employing various psychological constructs and measures, show the home-educated are developing at least as well, and often better than, those who attend institutional schools. No research contravenes this evidence. For example, regarding aspect of self-concept in the psychological development of children, several studies have revealed that the self-concept of homeschooled students is significantly higher than that of public school students. As another example, [Larry] Shyers found the only significant childhood social-interaction difference between the institutionally-schooled and homeschoolers was that the institutionally-schooled had higher problem behavior scores.

The second question related to socialization is how the homeschooled child will do in the "real world."

Preparedness for the "Real World"

Many define the "real world" as the world of adulthood, in which one is responsible for obtaining one's own food, shelter and clothing. For some college students, the "real world" is four years away. Others are already in the "real world," because, in addition to taking classes, they work to provide their own food and shelter. To simplify the matter for this article, the "real world" is defined as life after secondary school.

[H]omeschooled students demonstrated similar academic preparedness for college and similar academic achievement in college as students who had attended conventional schools.

Linda Montgomery, a principal of a private high school, was one of the first to look to the future and adulthood of the home-educated. She investigated the extent to which home-schooled students were experiencing conditions that foster leadership in children and adolescents who attend institutional schools. Her findings on 10- to 21-year-olds showed that the home-educated were certainly not isolated from social and group activities with other youth and adults. They were quite involved in youth group and other church activities, jobs, sports, summer camps, music lessons, and recitals. She concluded that homeschooling nurtured leadership at least as well as does the conventional system.

Homeschoolers' Self-Identity

Susannah Sheffer talked with homeschooled adolescent girls moving into adulthood. Sheffer began her report by citing the work of Carol Gilligan and her colleagues in the Harvard Project on Women's Psychology and Girls' Development who, lamenting, "have written about girls' 'loss of voice' and increasing distrust of their own perceptions." Sheffer suggested that the great difference in structure and function—the way things work, the relationships people have, expected behaviors, and the roles people play—between homeschooling and conventional schooling may have explained why she found so many of these home-educated adolescents to have not lost their voice and sense of identity. Meredith, a 14-year-old in

Sheffer's study, said, "I was worried that I would become a typical teenager if I went to school" and "I think some people would have seen [school] as my opportunity to 'be like everybody else.' But I didn't want to be like everybody else." Sheffer concluded, "Throughout this book the homeschooled girls I've interviewed have echoed these statements. They have talked about trusting themselves, pursuing their own goals, maintaining friendships even when their friends differ from them or disagree with them." Finally, these home-educated girls maintain their self-confidence as they pass into womanhood.

College Academic and Preparedness Predictors

Sheffer's findings regarding adolescent girls might explain some of the successes that other researchers have found, regarding young adults who were homeschooled. In a study that categorized college students as either home, public or private schooled, and examined their aptitude for achievement in college English, [Rhonda] Galloway and [Joe] Sutton found that homeschooled students demonstrated similar academic preparedness for college and similar academic achievement in college as students who had attended conventional schools. . . .

Similarly, [Paul] Jones and [Gene] Gloeckner cited three studies as showing the home-educated to be performing as well or better than institutional-school graduates at the college level. Jones and Gloeckner, in their own study, concluded, "The academic performance analyses indicate that home school graduates are as ready for college as traditional high school graduates and that they perform as well on national college assessment tests as traditional high school graduates".

Performance on College Admission Entrance Exams

ACTs and SATs are the best-known test predictors of success in university or college in America. Both the SAT and ACT publishers have reported for several years that the scores of the homeschooled are higher, on average, than those from public schools. For example, for the 1999-2000 school year, the home-educated scored an average of 568 in verbal while the state-school (i.e., public-school) average was 501, and 532 in math while the state-school average was 510.

Several colleges think so well of home-educated students that they have been actively recruiting them for several years.

Galloway and Sutton used academic, cognitive, spiritual, affective-social, and psychomotor criteria for measuring success at a private university. Among other things, they found that homeschooled students held significantly more positions of appointed and spiritual leadership, and had more semesters of leadership service than did those from private schools, and were statistically similar to the public school graduates.

College Admission Officers' Perceptions

Although some college and university personnel have shown animosity toward the homeschooling process, it appears that most are now interested in welcoming the home-educated. A recent survey asked many questions of 34 college admission officers in Ohio, who averaged 10 years of experience in college admission work and of whom 88 percent had personal experience working with homeschooled students. For example, they were asked how homeschooled students at their institution compared to their general student population in terms of academic success. About nine percent said "far more academically successful," 22 percent reported "somewhat more academically successful," 38 percent said "academically about average," zero percent reported "somewhat less academically successful," zero percent said "far less academically successful," and 31 percent said "don't know." On a five-point, strongly agree-strongly disagree scale, the admission officers were nearly symmetrical in their responses to the statement, "As the primary instructors, parents should be recognized as capable of evaluating their student's academic competence in letters of recommendation" (i.e., 32 percent agree, 24 percent neither, and 32 percent disagree). To the item, "The majority of homeschooled students are at least as socially well adjusted as are public schooled students," 44 percent agreed or strongly agreed, 35 percent responded "neither," and 21 percent disagreed or strongly disagreed. Likewise, Irene Prue's nationwide study of college admission personnel revealed that ". . . homeschoolers are academically, emotionally, and socially prepared to succeed in college."

College Recruitment

Several colleges think so well of home-educated students that they have been actively recruiting them for several years (e.g., Boston University, Nyack College). Christopher Klicka's survey of college admission officers found a Dartmouth College admission officer saying, "The applications [from homeschoolers] I've come across are outstanding. Homeschoolers have a distinct advantage because of the individualized instruction they have received." This individualized instruction, combined with homeschooled students' experience in studying and pursuing goals on their own, may be showing long-lasting effects. Admission officers at Stanford University think they are seeing an unusually high occurrence of a key ingredient, which they term "intellectual vitality," in homeschool graduates. They link it to the practice of self-teaching prevalent in these young people, as a result of their homeschool environment. . . .

How Colleges Approach the Home-Educated

Jennifer Sutton (2002) wrote in Brown University's alumni magazine, "Although the number of homeschoolers applying to college is still small, it represents only the first wave. The next homeschooled generation—the real boom—is just hitting puberty." *The Chronicle of Higher Education* headlined another article, "Homeschooling: Growing Force in Higher Education". Sixty-two percent of college admission officers agreed "the homeschool movement is having or will have a significant impact on higher education". As the number of home-schooled college applicants increases, college admission officers should keep the following in mind:

Research and probability show that the home-educated college applicant is very likely to succeed in college, both academically and socially. Consider that the home-educated typically have strong self-discipline, motivation, and self-initiative. "These kids are the epitome of Brown students," says Joyce Reed, who became an associate dean of the college twelve years ago. "They've learned to be self-directed, they take risks, they face challenges with total fervor, and they don't back off."

As with any applicant, you will need to use your wisdom and experience to determine whether the individual person fits the particular ethos of your institution, if "fit" is of high importance to your college.

Recognize that you may hold biases and prejudices you do not recognize. After all, about five American generations have been attending age-segregated, institutional places of learning for 12 years of our lives, and most reading this article spent at least 16 years in these institutions. Most Americans (and those in many other nations) have no idea of what it would be like to be home-educated and how we might be different, for better or worse, had we experienced this age-old practice.

Make sure your college has policies for receiving applications from and admitting the home-educated and make sure that your admission policies are reasonable, based on research and broad experience, and fair.

Here are some guidelines (some of which are from the Home School Legal Defense Association, 2004):

1. If your institution requires an SAT or ACT score in general, then simply also require that of the homeschooler.

2. Ask the home-educated to provide you with a transcript, but have flexible guidelines for these records and documentation of courses of study completed. They will not have the same look as those from institutional schools.

3. Ask the home-educated for a list of "extracurricular" activities.

4. Ask them for a bibliography of what they read during their secondary years. You might learn things about the breadth and depth of their education that you would have never known, especially if you only ask for a transcript.

5. Recognize the validity of homeschool high school completion or diplomas. Homeschooling is legal in all 50 states and, as explained in this article, the research shows that they are doing well academically.

6. For more information, contact the National Home Education Research Institute.

Homeschooling is growing and will continue to grow. Based on current information, there may be 3 million homeschool K-12 students living in the U.S. by 2010. Colleges and universities will soon see a sudden growth in the number applying for admission. Evidence to date points to a high success rate in adulthood in general, and in college in particular, for these individuals who have been raised and educated outside mainstream institutional schools. Perhaps they will bring, at a higher rate, some distinctive and positive traits to your college's or university's life that neither you nor professors have seen in awhile.

12

The Claim that Homeschool Students Excel Is Exaggerated

Dennis J. Willard and Doug Oplinger

Dennis J. Willard and Doug Oplinger are Akron Beacon Journal *staff writers.*

Anecdotes of stellar achievements, high test scores, and the reported results of national studies have won homeschoolers the respect of the majority of Americans and freedom from state and federal oversight. However, the test-writers and researchers behind the data complain that homeschool advocates have poorly analyzed and misrepresented it. Additionally, while homeschoolers have been admitted to prestigious universities, some college admissions officers report that the number of homeschooled applicants is negatively disproportionate to the estimated homeschool population.

Lack of Proof

Home-schooled children have won the National Spelling Bee twice and National Geography Bee three times in the last eight years.

Home-schooling parents point to college entrance-exam results as proof their children score higher than the general population.

Many home-schooled students are National Merit Scholars.

With victories such as those under their belts, plus an armload of data-driven studies, homeschooling parents argue that their children not only are succeeding academically, but also are doing far better than those in the public schools.

"Home schoolers have demonstrated significant academic achievement, and the Home School Legal Defense Association is unaware of any serious critics who still argue that home schoolers struggle academically," Michael Smith, president of the politically powerful HSLDA [Home School Legal Defense Association], wrote in a recent article.

Asked about the statement, Smith told the *Akron Beacon Journal* that anyone who suggests otherwise is "biased."

Indeed, there are many among the approximately 1.1 million home-schooled children who are receiving an above-average education.

However, if Americans accept the idea that home schooling is putting public schools to shame with an extraordinary crop of bright students, it's mainly because home schoolers successfully have marketed good anecdotes and bad analyses of the few national studies. . . .

Little State Accountability

At the same time the nation is collecting an unprecedented volume of statistics on public school students, their teachers and school buildings, it asks for almost nothing and knows almost nothing about children who are educated at home.

Home-schooling parents say that because they accept no tax dollars, they should be free of oversight.

Advocates validate their academic success with standardized test scores from a select group of home-schooled children, but they also argue against mandatory testing of all home schoolers because they believe the methodology is flawed and ignores their children's individuality. They decry the curricula imposed upon teachers to prepare children to pass the tests as a key reason for their opting to home-school.

"Is it fair that the state decides how you bring your child up? No, I don't think it is a good question," a home-schooling mother said in a *Beacon Journal* focus group that granted all its participants anonymity. "I think that infringes on our basic rights as Americans."

With few exceptions, most levels of government don't ask questions of the home-school population.

No Federal Accountability

The administration of President George W. Bush and Congress exempted home schoolers from the No Child Left Behind Act.

The No Child Left Behind law requires extensive testing in all public schools, while only 11 states, according to the Home School Legal Defense Association, have mandatory home-school testing. Most of those states don't require the parents to show the scores to school officials.

No Child Left Behind also imposes a costly requirement on schools to hire "highly qualified teachers," while many of the country's largest states have no requirements for parents wanting to home-school.

In Ohio, parents are given options as to how to show their children are succeeding. Most choose an "academic assessment" performed by a certified teacher and delivered to the local superintendent.

There is no requirement the assessing teacher talk to the child. Some of the assessors are immediate family members; some are not properly certified.

In one effort to show the assessments could be bogus, a Colorado man secured one through the mail for his dog. . . .

Dubious Conclusions

To deter calls for government oversight, home-schooling parents have presented colorful bar charts and studies to state lawmakers, sent information packets to the news media and posted reports on the Internet that suggest their children routinely outperform public school children.

However, the authors of the most prominent home-school research say that no study confirms that claim.

Lawrence M. Rudner published the pivotal study of home schooling in 1999. At the time, he was an independent education researcher at the University of Maryland.

As portrayed by home schoolers, the Rudner report suggested that children educated at home scored, on average, better than 70 percent to 80 percent of public school students and at least a grade level ahead.

Rudner's credentials gave his 1999 study special credibility. Even though HSLDA sponsored his work, he was identified as an "independent researcher" whose work was critiqued by peers.

To a nonresearcher looking at the report, the study was impressive because of its large sample of 20,000 children and its use of the well-known Iowa Tests of Basic Skills and the Tests of Achievement and Proficiency.

Today, however, Rudner said his work has been misrepresented. He said home schoolers are drawing incorrect conclusions, and newspaper reporters are quoting each other rather than reading what he wrote.

"The biggest annoyance was a large number of reporters that had read previous articles and never went to the original source and read the caveats," said Rudner, now chief psychometrician for the Graduate Management Admission Council, where he is responsible for guaranteeing the reliability of college testing.

Rudner wrote multiple cautionary statements in his report and, in interviews at the time, urged reporters not to make blanket comparisons with all public school children.

"This was not a controlled experiment," and it "does not demonstrate that home schooling is superior to public or private schools, and the results must be interpreted with caution," he wrote in the first paragraph of his report.

Misrepresentation of Study Results

Nonetheless, in the week following release of his study in March 1999, at least 20 stories in major U.S. newspapers referred in glowing terms to the success of home schoolers. "Study finds children schooled at home learn more," one headline read.

Some stories included Rudner's caveats; others did not.

The Daily Oklahoman, in an editorial, pointed out that Rudner's study was peer-reviewed—meaning that other researchers examined and commented on his work. The editorial, however, didn't mention that the peer who wrote the official review was highly critical of the study.

Kariane Mari Welner, a researcher at the University of California at Los Angeles at the time, wrote that there were basic problems with the group that Rudner surveyed, resulting in "an erroneous picture of home schooling." She criticized the "universal conclusions trumpeted by the HSLDA" that were beyond the reach of the study.

[I]f you took the same kids and the same parents and put them in the public schools, these kids would probably do exceptionally well.

HSLDA Chairman Michael Farris, who in 1999 was president of the organization, held a news conference at the time of the report's release to declare that the question of home-school academics had been proved to be a non-issue. He predicted the Rudner study would be used across the country as evidence that home schooling deserves less regulation, not more.

"We're doing well, and we've earned the right to have more and more freedom," Farris said in the *Virginian-Pilot*, a daily newspaper in Norfolk, Va. "People shouldn't be regulated where they don't need to be."

Misuse of Study Results

In dozens of states since then, the study has been used as evidence for relaxed home-school oversight or to fight off efforts to add regulations.

In the recent *Beacon Journal* interview, Rudner said his only conclusion was that if a homeschooling parent "is willing to put the time and energy and effort into it—and you have to be a rare person who is willing to do this—then in all likelihood you're going to have enormous success. I'll continue to say that."

He added: "I made the case in the paper that if you took the same kids and the same parents and put them in the public schools, these kids would probably do exceptionally well."

The main problem with the study, a number of critics said, is that participation was voluntary.

"Obviously, there is no point taking a test that you know you are going to fail," said Clive Belfield, a Columbia University education professor who also studies home schoolers.

Volunteers' results were compared with results from public schools, where all students must take the achievement tests, and where, under the No Child Left Behind Act, schools and teachers are judged by the results.

Nonetheless, home schoolers' interpretation of the Rudner study was accepted because no other study of its magnitude had been attempted. It changed the arguments about home schooling, Belfield said.

"He was the first mover on this. Before this, there was no story, basically. After Rudner, there is a story," Belfield said.

Admission-test Scores

The misuse of data and research also applies to college admissions.

Home schoolers generally score 8 percent to 9 percent higher on the SAT than public schoolers. Those scores are widely quoted in newspapers and in legislative hearings as proof of success.

However, representatives of both the SAT and ACT exams cautioned against drawing any conclusions from the numbers. They offered these reasons:

- Home schoolers appear to be underrepresented in the tests, raising questions about the number of home schoolers going to college.

- Some test takers who identify themselves as home-schooled say they have a ranking in their graduating class, which could indicate they were in a school rather than home-educated.

- Home schoolers who take the entrance tests are disproportionately white and from families with above-average income and education. This demographic group tends to score higher than the average anyway.

Belfield said it's inappropriate to compare ACT or SAT scores for a select group of home schoolers with those of all young people, just as it was in Rudner's study.

Home schoolers are enrolling and succeeding in universities, but it's not known whether they are doing so in numbers comparable to the general population.

Belfield obtained the 2001 SAT results, adjusted them for socio-economic characteristics and found the score gap was cut in half.

One could conclude, Belfield said, that good home-schooling situations result in better academic performance. But, he said, the fact that so few test takers are home schoolers continues to raise questions about whether they are going to college.

Numbers in College

Still, the anecdotes about home schoolers getting into top colleges have created an image of success for the entire movement.

"I've learned that you don't really need a diploma to get into college," a home-schooling mother said in a *Beacon Journal* focus group. "I've learned that the Ivy League schools actively go out and recruit home-school kids."

A newspaper in Alberta, Canada, reported last year: "With elite schools such as Harvard and Yale actively recruiting the home-schooled, home schooling's academic credentials are no longer in question."

Home schoolers are enrolling and succeeding in universities, but it's not known whether they are doing so in numbers comparable to the general population.

Dorie Baker, a spokeswoman for the dean of admissions for arts and humanities at Yale University, told the *Beacon Journal* that the dean was "surprised that anyone was asking" about home-schooled applicants because they are "so few and far between."

Officials at the University of Pennsylvania, an Ivy League school, told the *New York Times* in 1999 that 0.17 percent of their applicants were home schoolers, or about one-tenth the rate it should be to be proportionate with the estimated home-school population nationwide of about 2 percent. The Ohio Board of Regents, which handles data on all of Ohio's public universities and two-year colleges, a year ago found the same percentage as the University of Pennsylvania: 0.17 percent of incoming freshmen said they were home-schooled.

The U.S. Military Academy in West Point, N.Y., said that in the last five years, about 0.4 percent of its applicants were home-schooled, and only 0.3 percent of those admitted were home-schooled.

In a survey by the *Beacon Journal*, a few small Ohio colleges—notably Mount Vernon Nazarene and Findlay—

reported disproportionately large numbers of incoming freshmen who were home-schooled, but not enough to significantly affect Ohio's overall numbers.

Homeschool Advocates Respond

Michael Smith, president of the Home School Legal Defense Association, said there are some reasons for what appear to be low college-enrollment numbers.

In many major states, among them California, home schools are legally defined as private schools, he said.

Many states require those schools to have names or identification numbers, so that when the home-schooled student takes a national standardized test or enrolls in a college, he or she may be inclined to check the box for private school rather than home school, Smith said.

"Some of the colleges may be fudging a bit," too, he said. They're concerned that if they disclose admission of home-schooled young people who don't have high school diplomas, they may lose federal aid that targets high school graduates, he said.

And, Smith said, many home schoolers attend two-year colleges before they're 18 and move directly into four-year colleges without taking college admissions tests.

Last fall, the Home School Legal Defense Association released its own study that said homeschool graduates nationwide attend college at a far higher rate than a similar age group in the general population.

To achieve HSLDA's claim, the home-school enrollment rate would need to be 10 times what the Ohio Board of Regents, the University of Pennsylvania and the SAT and ACT testing services say their data show.

As in the Rudner study, the home-schooled participants in the HSLDA's study were volunteers and were compared with the general population. Half were full-time college students at the time. . . .

Success vs. Failure

The Beacon Journal interviewed nine researchers whose studies on home schooling are most often quoted. They have done original research and include representatives of Columbia and Stanford universities and the Education Commission for the States. They agreed: There is no statistical evidence that children who are kept home to be educated perform at a much higher level than public school students.

Yet in Congress, a bill—proposed in cooperation with the HSLDA—would give home schoolers more freedoms, access to federally funded college scholarships and protection from oversight.

The reason, the bill says, is because home schooling is successful.

"Education by parents at home has proven to be an effective means for young people to achieve success on standardized tests," the bill says, in part.

U.S. Rep. John Boehner, R-West Chester, one of the strongest proponents of collecting more data on public schools and holding them accountable under the No Child Left Behind Act, is one of the bill's co-sponsors.

But while everyone acknowledges there are failures, no one knows how many or where they are, and many school officials have no authority to challenge the parents.

A social worker in a *Beacon Journal* focus group said: "It is a problem even if it is a small minority group of children. We need to take care of those children, too. They can't take care of themselves."

Delaine Eastin, who was twice elected superintendent of California's public school system, said many home-schooling families are doing a wonderful job, but there were too many instances in her state where home-schooled 18-year-olds were illiterate.

At a time when No Child Left Behind is imposing financial penalties on states for falling short of goals, Eastin said, the federal and state governments are ignoring home schoolers.

"We're making such a fuss about accountability for some and no accountability for others," Eastin said. "Shouldn't we pay some attention to the home schoolers?"

13

Homeschooling Will Change the Future of Education

Robert Sanborn, Adolfo Santos, Alexandra L. Montgomery and James B. Caruthers

Robert Sanborn is the executive director of the Education Foundation of Harris County, Texas and a columnist on education and career topics for the Houston Post. *Adolfo Santos is professor of political science at the University of Houston-Downtown and is involved in evaluating education policy. Alexandra L. Montgomery is a graduate of the master's program in futures studies at the University of Houston-Clear Lake. She serves as a program coordinator for the Education Foundation of Harris County. James B. Caruthers is the communications coordinator for the Education Foundation of Harris County. He is currently working on a book about public education.*

Technology, immigration, alternative education, and school choice are forces that will change the face of education over the next twenty years. With these variables and others in play, it is impossible to truly predict the future; nevertheless, several visions have been conceived. Wireless technology will be harnessed to provide direct education from and to anywhere in the world through nodes attached to our brains. Homeschooling will become a status symbol and create an extreme social and economic divide between those who do and those who do not. Increased immigration will add to the social polarization creating two classes: the college educated and manual laborers. Special experi-

Robert Sanborn, Adolfo Santos, Alexandra L. Montgomery and James B. Caruthers, "Four Scenarios for the Future of Education," *The Futurist*, vol. 39, no. 1, January–February 2005, pp. 26–30. Reproduced by permission of The World Future Society.

ential schools, which stress social skills and instruction from ex-perts in the field who are not necessarily teacher certified, will give an edge to the students who attend them.

Many forces will act powerfully upon the course of public education in the future. Trends engendered by new technologies, immigration, school choice, and alternative education methods carry with them the muscle to reshape the form, content, and methods of education. Every competing interest wants time or money to solve the problem of education, and each is usually justified by some political, social, economic, moral, and/or philosophical reasoning. With so many forces at work, it seems unlikely that there is a single, predictable future for public education.

We believe, however, that it is possible to conceive of a number of realities that might exist at different points in the future. The following four futures for public education are alternative scenarios that might take place sometime in the next 20 years. Each future is independent within a broad spectrum of possible outcomes, making up a nonconsecutive timeline containing four separate scenarios based on our understanding of public education today as being volatile and in desperate need of change.

Scenario 1 (2012): Direct Education

By 2012, we can expect to see technology at every level of public education. Technological innovations such as implanted nodes will be attached to our brains through advances in non-invasive nanotechnology. Using Wi-Fi or Wi-Max, the nodes will access information from an advanced World Wide Web, and implants will be quite useful (sometimes essential) to learning. High-tech devices will offer school efficiency and transparency like never before.

In this scenario, we have harnessed technology to enable students and teachers to make giant leaps in education and information access. Technology not only encompasses computers and multimedia presentations, but also the very essence of how we educate, learn, and access information that we might have once considered too varied, weighty, and difficult to manage. This view of personal access to learning and education is called Direct Education and consists of the following components.

Continuous Accountability (CA) is a proven manner of showing students' success in taking advantage of these technological marvels and really learning. In Direct Education schools, there is no need for regularly scheduled tests; through CA, students are tested randomly at levels suitable to what they have studied. Educators know on a consistent basis how well students are doing and where to emphasize new learning. Parents are also updated electronically on students' progress and given suggestions on how to help students progress and overcome challenges.

> *[H]omeschooling is just another modern convenience to keep children where they can be safe and secure.*

The primary accessory of Direct Education is implanted information nodes. Direct Education offers a line of direct information visors for those with a less-organic feel for technology, although most of Direct Education schools are well adapted to the information society. Either way, learning is merely a thought away, as information flows from wireless networks directly into students' consciousness. Direct Education is for those districts adventurous enough to truly prepare students for the future.

The actual classroom is different for every age and for every student. Virtual classrooms can be joined wirelessly from home and enable access to and complete hands-on experiential education for every imaginable subject. Direct Education core classes available in 2012 include building your own best friend in a cyborg workshop, undersea welding, virtual tattoo and body art, Native American ritual dance, conversing with Freud and Jung, working inside an operating theater, firsthand experience of animal culture and pack mentality, and exploring America with Lewis and Clark.

Scenario 2 (2014): Homeschooling

In 2014, K-12 education will no longer be confined to four walls and a classroom. Education will take place in a variety of settings, including cyberspace and virtual reality.

In this scenario, everything in the home is automated (for those living in smart homes, of course), so homeschooling is just another modern convenience to keep children where they can be safe and secure. Everyday computers suffice as classrooms, and software takes care of all menial grading and record keeping.

Homeschooling grew in popularity as college-educated moms came to believe that public-school students were just test-takers and numbers for a head-count. For these moms, the official ways of measuring student intelligence and progress have long been debunked. Homeschool moms are adamant about one thing: They are far too informed to allow their children to participate in the manipulation of numbers as they relate to school performance and funding.

Parents are also concerned about special-needs children, another segment of the student population whose parents feel betrayed by false promises of equality in education. Upper-class moms of children with behavioral, developmental, or psychological challenges seem to prefer their own inexperienced but loving at-home care and instruction to the cold and impersonal shuffling their children received in public schools. The voucher and private school systems have failed, too, since taxpayer-funded vouchers did not accommodate the extra expense of special-needs programs. For the cost of private-school tuition, many parents turn instead to homeschooling, where they can bring in professional tutors, experts on their children's conditions, and consultants whose mastery exceeded anything public schools could offer.

The same society that lavishes worship on mothers who homeschool resents those who don't.

In many ways, homeschooling in 2014 has become a status symbol: Mothers who homeschool their children are thought of (and think of themselves) as highly sophisticated and well connected. A homeschool educator tends to rank high on levels of education attainment (master's degree or better) and household income (well into the upper brackets). Many well-to-do mothers revel in the feeling of staying home with children. Savvy domestic skills, maturity, and intelligence are the ideal of contemporary motherhood, something no mother who works outside the home could accomplish.

There is an extreme polarity between the homeschooled and public-schooled. While personal, loving attention is bestowed upon one group, the other is reduced to being a test score in a government-monitored database. Homeschooled children are well rounded and have refined interests; public-school graduates have been stifled and processed through an impersonal and degrading system. Colleges and society accept both types, though there is a noticeable difference in the values and work styles of each.

The same society that lavishes worship on mothers who homeschool resents those who don't. While there may be a different type of liberation in the homeschool revolution (one that reveres mothers), there is a backlash against parenting that is not seen as selfless, particularly when it comes to educating one's child.

Moreover, nontraditional families and poor families are considered inadequate for the whole enrichment of a child. Though fathers play minor parts in the homeschool phenomena, their presence is mandatory. Homeschool moms consider it their life's work, but there is no financial reward. It is truly a labor of love—and a signal of certain elevated social status.

Scenario 3 (2020): Generations Left Behind

A poor, uneducated workforce—made up of new immigrants, dropouts from immigrant families, and the urban poor of all ethnicities—will become trapped in low-paying, menial jobs with no real opportunity for advancement. In 2020, there will be two distinctly disparate social segments: college-educated information pushers who work in the top and middle corporate echelons and manual laborers with corresponding demarcations in race and status. In other words, a class system based on education levels will have developed.

In this scenario, the United States has become helplessly polarized, and other segments of society (such as middle- and upper-class Anglo- and African-Americans) have grown resentful of the amount of national resources being used to improve the prospects for first-generation Americans.

Among immigrant populations, a sense of alienation pervades, and social assimilation levels continue to decline. In tandem, the quality of public education in urban areas continues to drop, and though mighty efforts have been made to get high-school graduates from poor-performing sectors into college, they lack the academic skills to survive once they arrive there.

Since the beginning of the twenty-first century, larger family households and lower incomes have compelled too many first-generation Americans to put less emphasis on education and more on sending youth into the workforce as soon as possible. Add up the variables two decades later, and that is how the United States in 2020 has created a Third-World workforce.

Scenario 4 (2025): Experiential Schools

By 2025, a combination of nontraditional and tried-and-true techniques will generate a new kind of expertise in the classroom. Research shows that experiential education—focusing on enriching social skills and interpersonal relationships—works best for student satisfaction, interest, engagement, and retention. In 2025, students at a typical experiential school will place in the top percentage nationally, with nearly all graduates either going directly to college or entering the workforce as skilled workers.

In this scenario, all experiential-school students receive the fundamentals required of high-school graduates at the beginning of the century, including language skills, math, sciences, and history. But in 2025, these basics are now delivered by an entirely new approach to instruction and with a great deal more effectiveness. One way is through a "master teacher" program, where distinguished experts in every field come to the classroom, bringing their years of education and experience to work teaching the basics. A retired statistician from a prestigious research firm, say, might teach math, outlining course material, giving broad concepts, and explaining theory. After she's finished lecturing, the class divides into smaller groups, tended by teaching staff circulating around the room to help students assimilate and apply what they've just learned.

A nutritionist with a degree in sports medicine might be the master teacher in the physical education department. Students learn healthy lifestyles as well as enjoy an exercise program designed to keep them active and interested in maintaining good health. Thanks to legislation relaxing teacher certification guidelines, experiential schools are able to bring in people from the community with degrees specifically related to the fields they teach and considerable "real world" experience. Furthermore, through these sessions, students who grasp the material more quickly are encouraged to assist their peers.

At the experiential school, community involvement is paramount. A separate board, composed of parents, has considerable input in school decisions. A trained mediator is also on staff to help all branches of school government interact smoothly. Political firestorms are circumvented because the schools emphasize a solid foundation in key subject areas without interference from political agenda pushers. . . .

Our Vision

A vision is the future that we would most like to see take place. Our vision reflects the values we wish to convey to the rest of the world—how we think the future should be. Alternative futures can be visions, but they can be strategic, too. As our priorities and resources change, so will our perception of public education.

Organizations to Contact

The editors have compiled the following list of organizations concerned with the issues debated in this book. The descriptions are derived from materials provided by the organizations. All have publications or information available for interested readers. The list was compiled on the date of publication of the present volume; the information provided here may change. Be aware that many organizations take several weeks or longer to respond to inquiries, so allow as much time as possible.

American Homeschool Association
P.O. Box 3142, Palmer, AK   99645
(800) 236-3278
e-mail: aha@americanhomeschoolassociation.org
Web site: www.americanhomeschoolassociation.org

The AHA was created to network homeschoolers on a national level. Current AHA services include an online news and discussion list, which provides news, information, and resources for homeschooling families.

Education Law Association
300 College Park-0528, Dayton, OH   45469
(937) 229-3589
e-mail: ela@educationlaw.org
Web site: www.educationlaw.org

ELA is a nonprofit, non-advocacy organization open to anyone interested in education law. They provide unbiased information about current legal issues affecting education in schools, colleges, and universities, and have been doing so since they were founded at the time of the Brown v. Board of Education decision in 1954.

Home School Legal Defense Association (HSLDA)
P.O. Box 3000, Purcelville, VA   20134

(540) 338-5600
e-mail: info@hslda.org
Web site: www.hslda.org

HSLDA is a Christian organization of homeschooling families. The association's goal is to defend and advance the constitutional right of parents to direct the education of their children and to protect family freedoms. It supports homeschooling families by negotiating with local officials, serving as an advocate in court proceedings, monitoring federal legislation, and fighting any proposed laws seen as harmful.

National African-American Homeschooling Alliance
e-mail: info@naaha.com
Web site: www.naaha.com

The NAAHA began from a desire to unite African-American homeschoolers nationally. Launched in January 2003, NAAHA is a nonsectarian organization where all families' religious values are appreciated and welcomed.

National Center for Education Statistics (NCES)
1990 K St. NW, Washington, DC   20006
(202) 502-7300
Web site: http://nces.ed.gov

NCES is part of the U.S. Department of Education and serves as the primary federal entity for collecting and analyzing data related to education in the United States and other countries. The center organizes training seminars, holds conferences, and publishes its findings in reports and in its publications, including the *Education Statistics Quarterly* and the *Digest of Education Statistics*.

National Education Association
1201 16th St. NW, Washington, DC   20036
(202) 833-4000
Web site: www.nea.org

The NEA is a volunteer-based organization whose goal is to advance the cause of public education. The association lobbies legislators for school resources, campaigns for higher standards for the teaching profession, and files legal actions to protect academic freedom. At the local level, the association conducts professional workshops and negotiates contracts for school district employees.

National Home Education Network
P.O. Box 7844, Long Beach, CA   90807
e-mail: info@nhen.org
Web site: www.nhen.org

The NHEN exists to encourage and facilitate the grassroots work of state and local homeschooling organizations and individuals by providing information, fostering networking and promoting public relations on a national level.

National Home Education Research Institute
P.O. Box 13939, Salem, OR   97309
(503) 364-1490
e-mail: mail@nheri.org
Web site: www.nheri.org

NHERI is a nonprofit research organization which collects, tracks, and analyzes research on home-based education. It seeks to educate the public about homeschool research through speaking engagements and through its publication of the *Home School Researcher*.

National School Boards Association
1680 Duke St., Alexandria, VA   22314
(703) 838-6722
e-mail: info@nsba.org
Web site: www.nsba.org

The NSBA serves the national and federal needs of local school boards. The association seeks to raise awareness of school board issues, assists school boards and educators in the uses

of technology, reports the results of research on education issues, and lobbies Congress. The NSBA publishes the monthly
magazine *American School Board Journal* and *The School Board
News*, a semi-monthly newspaper.

United States Department of Education
400 Maryland Ave. SW, Washington, DC   20202-0498
(800) USA-LEARN (1-800-872-5327)
e-mail: customerservice@inet.ed.gov
Web site: www.ed.gov

The purpose of the U.S. Department of Education is to ensure
equal access to education and to promote educational excel-
lence. The department provides grants to primary, secondary,
and post-secondary education institutes; financial aid to students for post-secondary education; and underwrites education research. It produces hundreds of publications annually,
including *Community Update*, which informs readers about
available resources, services, and publications.

United States Fund for UNICEF
333 East 38th Street, New York, NY   10016
(800) 4UN-ICEF (1-800-486-4233)
e-mail: information@unicefusa.org
Web sites: www.unicefusa.org

The United Nations Children's Fund, or UNICEF, is mandated
by the United Nations General Assembly to advocate for the
protection of children's rights, to help meet their basic needs,
and to expand their opportunities to reach their full potential.
UNICEF is guided by the Convention on the Rights of the
Child and strives to establish children's rights as enduring
ethical principles and international standards of behavior toward children.

Bibliography

Books

Michael W. Apple — *Educating the 'Right' Way: Markets, Standards, God, and Inequality*, 2nd ed. New York: Routledge, Taylor & Francis Group, 2006.

Bruce S. Cooper — *Home Schooling in Full View: A Reader*. Greenwich, CT: Information Age, 2005.

Mimi Davis — *So WHY Do You Homeschool?* Longwood, FL: Xulon Press, 2005.

David d'Escoto & Kim d'Escoto — *The Little Book of Big Reasons to Homeschool*. Nashville, TN: B & H Publishing Group, 2007.

Greg Dimitriadis, Dennis Carlson, & Simon Casey — *Promises to Keep: Cultural Studies, Democratic Education, and Public Life*. New York: RoutledgeFalmer, 2003.

Rachel Gathercole — *The Well-Adjusted Child: The Social Benefits of Homeschooling*. Highlands Ranch, CO: Mapletree, 2007.

Michelle Goldberg — *Kingdom Coming: The Rise of Christian Nationalism*, New York, W. W. Norton, 2006.

Angelina Hart — *Shouldn't You Be In School?* Charleston, SC: BookSurge, 2006.

John Holt and
Patrick Farenga
: *Teach Your Own: The John Holt Book of Homeschooling.* Cambridge, MA: Perseus Books, 2003.

H. M. Levin and
C. R. Belfield
: "The Marketplace in Education," *Review of Research in Education*, 2004, pp. 183–219.

Brian D. Ray
: *Worldwide Guide to Homeschooling, 2005–2006: Facts and Stats on the Benefits of Home School.* Nashville, TN: Broadman & Holman, 2005.

Rob Reich
: *Bridging Liberalism and Multiculturalism in American Education.* Chicago: University of Chicago Press, 2002.

Bruce N. Shortt
: *The Harsh Truth About Public Schools.* Vallecito, CA: Chalcedon/ Ross House Books, 2004.

Joel Turtel
: *Public Schools, Public Menace: How Public Schools Lie to Parents and Betray Our Children.* New York: Liberty Books, 2005.

Periodicals

Kurt J. Bauman
: "Home Schooling in the United States: Trends and Characteristics," *Education Policy Analysis*, May 16, 2002.

Michelle Conlin
: "Meet My Teachers: Mom and Dad," *Business Week, Student Edition*, February 20, 2006.

Michael P. Farris	"Can America Protect Parental Rights?" *The Home School Court Report*, November–December 2006.
Leslie Fulbright	"Blacks Take Education into Their Own Hands," *San Francisco Chronicle*, September 25, 2006.
Paul Jones and Gene Gloeckner	"First-Year College Performance: A Study of Home School Graduates and Traditional School Graduates," *The Journal of College Admission*, Spring 2004.
Paul Jones and Gene Gloeckner	"A Study of Admission Officers' Perceptions of and Attitudes toward Homeschool Students," *Journal of College Admission*, Fall 2004.
The Journal of Blacks in Higher Education	"Now Home-Schooled Black Children Perform as Well as Home-Schooled Whites," Spring 2005.
Christopher J. Klicka	"Homeschooling Under Fire around the Country," *Practical Homeschooling*, January–February 2005.
Christopher J. Klicka	"Homeschool Graduates Enlisting in the Military are Protected," *Practical Homeschooling*, May–June 2006.
Chris Lubienski	"A Critical View of Home Education," *Evaluation and Research in Education*, 2003.
Wendy McElroy	"Can a Feminist Homeschool Her Child?" *Ideas on Liberty*, February 2002.

Daniel Monk   "Home Education: A Human Right?"
                     Evaluation and Research in Education,
                     2003.

Richard Morgan   "A Growing Force: In Fight for Fed-
                     eral Student Aid, Home-School
                     Lobby has Powerful Friends," *The
                     Chronicle of Higher Education*, Janu-
                     ary 17, 2003.

Nafisa M. Rachid   "Homeschooling; It's a Growing
                     Trend Among Blacks," *Network Jour-
                     nal*, February 2005.

Rob Reich   "The Civic Perils of Homeschooling,"
                     Educational Leadership, April 2002.

Rob Reich   "Opting Out of Education: Yoder,
                     Mozert, and the Autonomy of Chil-
                     dren," *Educational Theory*, Fall 2002.

Michael H.   "Revisiting the Common Myths
Romanowski   about Homeschooling," *The Clearing
                     House*, January–February 2006.

Kima Payne   "The Impact of Home Schooling
Stewart and   Regulations on Educational Enroll-
Richard A. Neeley   ments in the United States," *Educa-
                     tion*, Winter 2005.

Dennis J. Willard   "Home Schoolers' Motivations are
and Doug   Diverse; Their Teaching Styles Vary,"
Oplinger   *Akron Beacon Journal*, November 14,
                     2004.

Dennis J. Willard   "Home-schooling Freedoms Help
and Doug   Parents Who Abduct Children," *Ak-
Oplinger   ron Beacon Journal*, November 18,
                     2004.

Mary Ann Zehr   "More Home Schoolers Taking Advanced Placement Tests," *Education Week*, April 26, 2006.

Internet Sources

Clive R. Belfield   "Modeling School Choice: A Comparison of Public, Private-Independent, Private-Religious and Home-Schooled Students," *National Center for the Study of Privatization in Education*, Occasional Paper 49, June 2002. http://ncspe.org.

Clive R. Belfield   "Home-Schooling in the US," *National Center for the Study of Privatization in Education*, Occasional Paper 88, January 2004. http://ncspe.org.

Clearinghouse on Educational Policy and Management   *Trends and Issues: School Choice*, 2002. http://eric.uoregon.edu.

Eric Isenberg   "Home Schooling: School Choice and Women's Time Use," *National Center for the Study of Privatization in Education*, Occasional Paper 64, December 2002. http://ncspe.org.

Philip P. Kelly   "Educational Neglect & Compulsory Schooling in Idaho: 13,954 Reasons to Take Action, 2004–2005," *Center for School Improvement and Policy Studies, Boise State University*, 2006. http://csi.boisestate.edu.

National Center for Educational Statistics, U.S. Department of Education

Homeschooling in the United States: 2003 , February 2006. http://nces.ed.gov.

National Center for Educational Statistics, U.S. Department of Education

Issue Brief: 1.1 Million Homeschooled Students in the United States in 2003, July 2004. http://nces.ed.gov.

Brian D. Ray

"Homeschooling Grows Up," *Home School Legal Defense Association*, 2003. http://www.hslda.org.

Christine Scheller

"The Little School in the Living Room Grows Up," *Christianity Today*, September 9, 2002. http://ctlibrary.com.

United Nations International Children's Fund (UNICEF)

Fact Sheet: A Summary of the Rights Under the Convention on the Rights of the Child, 1990. www.unicef.org.

Bob Unruh

"Government Declares War on Homeschooling Parents," *WorldNetDaily*, December 21, 2006. www.wnd.com.

John T. Wenders and Andrea D. Clements

"Homeschooling in Nevada: The Budgetary Impact," *Nevada Research Policy Institute*, April 1, 2005. www.npri.org.

Index

A

Akron Beacon Journal (newspaper), 7, 89, 93, 97
Anecdotes
  homeschool advocates rely on, 39–40, 89
  on success of homeschoolers, 71–72, 76–77
Arnold, Dave, 75

B

Bastiat, Frederic, 47
Boehner, John, 97
Bush, George W., 90

C

Canada, homeschooling in, 11–12
Christianity Today (magazine), 18
Chronicle of Higher Education (journal), 86
College
  data is scarce on homeschooled students performance in, 95–96
  homeschooled students excel in, 79–87
Conners, Diane, 45
Continuous Accountability (CA), 101
Convention on the Rights of the Child, 8

D

Daily Oklahoman (newspaper), 92
Data
  on homeschooled students in college, is scarce, 95–96
  on homeschooling is imprecise, 38–40
Democracy
  homeschooling does not endanger, 25–28
  homeschooling endangers, 16–24
  protects individual freedom, 34, 35
Department of Education, U.S., 38
Direct Education, 100–102
Dobson, James, 17–18
Dobson, Linda, 74

E

Eastin, Delaine, 98
Eclectic Readers (McGuffey), 19
Education, public
  condemnation of, by Religious Right, 17–18
  homeschooling will change future of, 99–106
  importance of, 18–20
  states' responsibility for regulating, 29–30
Evaluation and Research in Education (journal), 13
Evangelical Christians
  in homeschool movement, 73–74
  views on public schools, 16–18
Experimental schools, 105–106

F

Families
  benefit from state-funded partnerships with homeschoolers, 48–52

homeschooling benefits, 53–57

homeschooling is not right for all, 58–63

Feminism, homeschooling is act of, 63–69

Fritz, Marshall, 18

G

Galloway, David, 14

Germany, ban on homeschooling in, 7–8, 14–15

Gillian, Carol, 82

Great Britain, reasons for homeschooling in, 13

Guenther, Richard, 14

H

Hartford Courant (newspaper), 45

Heritage Foundation, 18–19

Home Education Magazine, 74

Home School Legal Defense Association (HSLDA), 30, 96

Homeschool movement, history of, 73–74

Homeschoolers' Success Stories (Dobson), 74

Homeschooling

benefits families, 53–57

debate over, 31–32

democracy is endangered by, 16–24

democracy is not endangered by, 25–28

as feminist act, 63–69

is becoming more common around the world, 10–15

lack of state/federal accountability for, 89–90

reasons for, 54–55, 74–75

support for, 74–76

will change future of education, 99–106

hooks, bell, 36–37

J

Jackson, Jesse, Jr., 8

Jackson, Sheldon, 19

Japan, homeschooling in, 12–13

Johnson, Sonia, 65

K

Kamiyo, Hiroshi, 13

Knowles, J.G., 27

Kozol, Jonathan, 21

L

Lewis, SAmuel, 19

M

McGuffey, William Holmes, 19

Montgomery, Linda, 82

N

National Center for Education Statistics (NCES), 7

National Education Association (NEA), 44

National Home Education Network (NHEN), 30

New York Times Magazine, 21

No Child Left Behind Act (2001), 21, 90

O

Oakland Tribune (newspaper), 47

P

Paradis, John, 45

Partnerships, homeschool, benefit public schools/families, 48–51

Public schools
   justification of homeschooling due to failure of, is a red herring, 31
   societal affects of abandonment of, 20
   support for homeschoolers from, 75
   in U.S. history, 19
   views of evangelical Christians on, 16–18

R

Regulation, of homeschooling
   argument against, 43–47
   arguments for, 30–31, 32–38
   proposed framework for, 40–41
Religion, as reason for homeschooling, 13, 16–17, 73–74
Rothermel, Paula, 13, 14
Rudner, Lawrence M., 75–76, 91–92
Ryan, Don, 46

S

Schlessinger, Laura, 18
Self-identity, is maintained among homeschooled students, 82–83
Sheffer, Susanna, 82, 83
Slatter, Ian, 72, 74–75
Smith, J. Michael, 46–47, 89
Socialization
   homeschooling does not impact, 57, 81–82
   may be impacted by homeschooling, 36
Special-needs children, 102–103

Staples, Cameron, 45
Students, homeschooled
   are active in civic/political affairs, 26–27
   claims of academic success for, are exaggerated, 88–98
   excel in college, 79–87
   excel in national competitions, 70–78
   numbers of, 7, 38, 79
Surveys
   on public school support for homeschoolers, 75
   on reasons for homeschooling, 13
Sutton, Jennifer, 85

T

Time (magazine), 25
Trinity School, 19

U

UNICEF (United Nations International Children's Emergency Fund), 8

V

Virginian-Pilot (newspaper), 92
Vouchers, school, 21, 22
   have failed, 102
   Supreme Court's approval of, 23

W

Weaver, Reg, 22
Welner, Kariane Mari, 92